What other's are saying about
Drink Less, Be More

"This is such an important book. Not only does it provide practical tools for women to moderate and use alcohol safely it does so with humour, grace and where possible evidence based tips grounded in science." Meaghan Thumath, RN, BScN, MSc Public Health

"Reading 'Drink less be more' is like having a needed heart-to-heart with a good friend; to make those drinking changes we haven't been able to do alone. Offering practical guidance, other women's stories, ongoing support and a bit of tough love, this guide will help you finally reach your goal of moderate drinking." -Jillian Kowalchuk, MSc

"Caitlin's guide, "Drink Less, Be More" is a life-saver. She shows that it IS possible to have it all – to be a fun person, to enjoy your nights out, to enjoy a drink but with moderation and self-care, and to put let this self-care, and self-love and self-respect, as paramount. Caitlin shows how it IS possible to still be at the party but never again have a morning filled with regret or sad- ness or illness, and instead to let your life become one where you can fully trust yourself and enjoy yourself and always be in control and safe. I love it! I think it's necessary reading for us all!" - Aoife O'Leary

"Our relationships with alcohol may not fit into the box of alcoholism or problematic alcohol use, yet there are many times when we look ourselves in the mirror and wonder if we are happy with the way alcohol fits into our lives. Abstinence, although brilliant for some, may not be the solution for everyone. Drink Less Be More is a step by step guidebook for those whose hustle leads them to lean on alcohol too often.

No matter where you find yourself on the spectrum, Caitlin Padgett provides you with a starting place to reflect on "your body, your health, and your well-being" and to holistically improve your relationship with alcohol. She will take you through an approach of applying the strategies that work best for you; because after all, YOU are the reader and you are the one in control. And with time, your journey towards a healthier future will lead you to 'drinking less and living more.'" Natalie Chan - MD

"I used to dread going out to bars with my girlfriends because I was afraid of how I would feel the following morning- hungover and hating myself for not having the self-control. Now that I have read Caitlin's book Drink Less, Be More, I know what to do in situations involving alcohol. The tips are so useful and you can't find them anywhere else! I've shared these tips with my girlfriends/sip sisters and now we can all go out and have fun with no regrets. Thanks Caitlin!" - Nyssa Tan, RN, CHC

"In today's age of constant excesses to fill spiritual voids, Caitlin Padgett's book offers a refreshing approach. "Drink Less Be More" is full of sound advice for the modern woman on how to take make healthier decisions around drinking and take better care of the mind, body and soul. She aims not just to help women eliminate unhealthy behaviors but to be the fullest, brightest version of ourselves we can be.

As a physician working in the field of addiction, I am always interested in providing my patients with a spectrum of options. Sobriety and abstinence are the necessary for people with severe alcohol use disorders but are not always the best choice for the majority of women who struggle with alcohol's problematic effects.

Drink Less Be More offers an innovative and alternative approach to alcohol moderation from a woman who not only "gets it" from her personal experience but using scientific evidence and client testimonials as well." - Aleka MD

"Caitlin Padgett's book Drink Less, Be More has transformed the way I think about social drinking. She truly gives all the tools anyone would need to conquer their problematic drinking habits once and for all. This books inspired and supported me to feel my best when out with friends without needing to rely on alcohol. I've discovered the confidence to be myself and have even more fun than I ever thought was possible." - Heather Wise, MPH

"I knew alcohol was causing problems in my life, but I also knew didn't want to quit forever. Instead, I wanted to take a break, explore my relationship with it, and understand why it was a problem. Moreover, I wanted strategies to deal with it, within the larger picture of my life.

Drink Less Be More is the only book I can find that spoke to me. There's a spectrum that doesn't often get talked about, from a healthy drinker with no associated problems to an alcoholic. There is a whole number of people that fit somewhere in between, like me, and Caitlin gets that. It is not always easy to reflect deeply on your relationship with alcohol, and not unlike other vices, like food, it takes time to undo habits that have taken 20 years to form.

You need to start somewhere and this guide is the perfect place. Having Caitlin as my coach and this book as a guide has worked for me! I highly recommend it to anyone who wants a new approach and has been afraid to start the journey of redefining their relationship with alcohol ." - Claire

DRINK LESS BE MORE

DRINK LESS BE MORE

How to have a great night (and life!) without getting wasted

Caitlin Padgett

Cover Design: Nicole Farley

Cover Photo: Brandy Svendson, Brandyland Photography

ISBN: 1517792770
ISBN 13: 9781517792770
Library of Congress Control Number: 2015916901
CreateSpace Independent Publishing Platform
North Charleston, South Carolina

Dedication

To my Sip Sisters who have journey here with me, turning our wild ways into wisdom. Thank you for standing next to me without judgement - you know who you are.

To my mentors who encouraged me to shine brighter, and stay true, always.

Introduction

Have you ever woken up after a night out, struggling to recall the details? Or worse, with massive gaps in what you remember?

With a knot of underlying anxiety or guilt, worried about having done something you can guarantee you never would have done if you had had less to drink...or worried about something you "sort of" remember which you wish never happened?

Trying to swallow waves of nausea and dizziness, so that those around you won't notice how dysfunctional you feel?

With lingering foggy brain and a pounding between your temples, making it harder to concentrate and feel productive?

Thinking to yourself !@$)(*#@) "not again!!", why? What is wrong with me?

Swearing or praying up and down that this was the last time, that you will not drink like that ever again - even though you've made that same promise to yourself time and time again?

If you've found yourself saying "yes, that's me" to any of the questions above, you are certainly not alone.

I began asking questions about this topic while I was studying interdisciplinary humanities and psychology at the New College in San Francisco. I was so interested that I conducted a qualitative study of the relationship my female peers had with alcohol.

Since then, through conversations with friends, colleagues from public health policy, media and social awareness campaigns, fitness and health coaching, fashion and, of course, my clients, more women than not have at least one "whoops" moment with alcohol.

According to a study conducted by the US Center for Disease Prevention and Control in 2013, binge drinking - defined for women as four or more drinks in roughly two hours—is on the rise among American women, with one in eight drinking to excess three times per month.

I certainly used to fit that category, and have said yes to the questions above, many times over...more than I even care (or am able) to recall.

In fact, I lived this experience off and on for more than 15 years. I had my first blackout at age 16 and by age 30 still didn't have a handle on how to have a great night out and remember all the details. I needed to learn how to let go and have fun, without getting totally wasted.

The formula for my drunkenly wild nights out was embedded in me for as long as I can remember; it became like second nature. Learning how to dial back on the drinking was hard and took practice. It was like learning a new skill that required major shifts not only in my behaviour, but in my beliefs about myself.

During the years I was trying to get a handle on it all, I searched for resources directed at "someone like me." Someone who still wanted to go out and have fun, be able to drink one drink and stop there (or maybe drink none at all), and not cross (or stumble... or crash) over the line into oblivion or regret.

Despite my best efforts, I couldn't find many resources for women like me and my friends who were also struggling with the same issues.

My friends and I are all smart, educated, motivated and fun-loving people. We want to control our alcohol use so that it didn't control us, and so we don't have to quit completely, if we don't want to.

We are women who want to reflect our best selves to the world, day and night.

We also want to have a great night out - let loose, make a great impression, have fun and either make it home at a decent time or dance the night away without getting wasted. We want to know when to stop, (or not have any alcohol at all and not have it be a big deal). We want to be productive in the morning, feel great and remember everything the day after.

While there are plenty of resources for seeking sobriety or wanting to try abstinence, there are <u>very few</u> that teach us moderation, learning to drink without quitting, when in fact moderation is a strategy that can work for the majority of those who may have a 'problem' with alcohol. In fact, the Center for Disease Control and Prevention reports that most excessive drinkers (90%) did not meet the criteria for alcohol dependence.

✳ Moderation, simply put, is the avoidance of extremes or excesses... the "middle way" of alcohol management.

Buddha describes the middle way as a path of moderation, between the extremes of sensual indulgence and self-mortification (self-punishment). This, according to him, was the path of wisdom. It is also the path of ongoing effort.

The middle way could be framed another way, as a path of deep self-exploration. "The middle is messy, but it's also where the magic happens" as Brene Brown write in her new book, "Rising Strong". The middle way of moderation is amorphous; the boundaries are not so clearly defined. There is more wiggle room when you create your own rules.

The key with this approach is to go deeper than somebody else's information, such as focusing exactly on how many drinks to drink. Wisdom is the ability to think and act based on knowledge, but also experience, understanding and insight. My intention with this guide is to help you turn inward to figure out what unique approach will work for you, and only you. Alcohol and its 'problems' are not uniform; they are unique, like you— and the solution and strategies should also be unique to you.

––––––

A LITTLE BIT ABOUT ME

Looking back, it is hard for me to place exactly where I became a person that "drank too much." I started drinking around age 14 or 15, but the first time I got completely blackout wasted was when I was 16.

The only "education" I remember receiving in high school was a "just say no" approach, that didn't really give any in-depth information about alcohol's effects (and if it did, it clearly didn't have a lasting impact as I have zero recollection of it). Where I grew up, we were never taught about moderation or strategies to avoid getting "too drunk". We were just supposed to avoid alcohol altogether. Yet by my mid-teens, pretty much everyone I knew was drinking and knew where to get alcohol.

I used alcohol for confidence, to explore my sexuality, to deal with the stress of a turbulent time with my family, to have fun, and to forget my worries.

By the time I was 18, I was living in the city and working in nightclubs and after-hours parties from Thursday night to Sunday morning, even though I was underage. At the same time, I was working for a government-funded community program, as a youth facilitator. I learned very quickly that I could live two lives, one of Monday-Friday responsibility, and total "freedom" on the weekends.

My 20's were fast-paced, challenging and for the most part, really exciting. I certainly wouldn't have described myself as someone with a drinking problem. Yes, sometimes I drank too much and couldn't remember the details, but didn't we all?

I was still productive, wasn't I? I had accomplished so much at a young age. And besides, I always seemed to date people whose drug and alcohol problems were worse than mine.

Until I didn't.

At the end of my 20's I found myself getting a divorce from someone who had looked in my eyes and said, "Caitlin, when you drink you disappear."

I had tried a year and a half of sobriety, but had gone back to hard partying. I loved the release, the ability to let it all go.

By the time my 30th birthday rolled around, I had a nasty wake up call that literally smacked me right in the forehead. I drank so much that I fell and hit my forehead so hard on the concrete that I woke up with a giant goose egg staring back at me in the morning. I tried to laugh it off, but I knew something had to change.

I wish that I could say my drinking habits changed then and there, but they didn't. A year later I found myself at my 31st birthday, passed out after drinking too much absinthe.

Several weeks before my 32nd birthday, I finally decided enough was enough. After another wild night out, I woke up painfully hungover and trying to piece together the night before. I was absolutely sick - not only from the physical symptoms, but because I was so done with repeating the same pattern, over and over again. The next day, I vowed I would never be drunk again, and I haven't been.

For the following two years, I experimented with both moderation and sobriety. I became super tuned in to both my body and my mental, emotional and spiritual well-being, which serve as my internal compass. Carving this path for myself hasn't always been easy and there were definitely times I felt like giving up. I didn't let myself, and with the support and strategies described in this guide, I was able to persevere and thrive.

I now feel stronger, clearer and healthier than I ever have in my adult life.

- Instead of spending copious amounts on bottles of wine, bubbly and cocktails - I spend money on delicious, nourishing food.
- Instead of hazy hungover mornings turning into wasted days - I wake up with energy, clarity and enthusiasm.

- Instead of numbing stress, anxiety or accumulative shame - I feel and I deal, and I know that I can handle whatever comes my way.
- Instead of intimacy instigated with liquid courage - I have deeply meaningful intimate relationships (not to mention some of the best sex of my life - and I remember every moment).
- Instead of "pre-gaming" with my girlfriends by downing a bottle (or two) of bubbly before even heading out the door - I am present and aware of how I am feeling and enjoy alcohol free bubbly treats as I get ready.
- Instead of feeling stuck in a job that wasn't fulfilling - I have created a life for myself that combines my passions, skills and talents.

I dedicated myself full time to healing, learning and growing. I enrolled in the Institute for Integrative Nutrition to become a Holistic Health Coach, and once certified, began coaching others who were going through similar struggles.

As a coach who supports clients to get a handle on their alcohol use, to feel better in their bodies, and live their lives to the fullest, I draw from a variety of tools and techniques that are grounded in the concepts of bio-individuality (each person is unique and requires their own approach), holistic health and healing, my background in dance and fitness, and over 10 years working in health policy.

I have created the life of my dreams. Since those pivotal moments several years ago, I have stepped fully into myself and as a result, wake up with joy and gratitude daily. I want this for you too, which is why I created this guide.

WHO THIS GUIDE IS FOR
This guide is for anyone who wants to have a different relationship with alcohol - one that **you** control - and live your best life: full of fun, adventure,

passion, and, of course, better health. "Drinking less" and your relationship with alcohol is defined by you, not by me. Whether your goal is to have one less drink a night, to remember all the details, to never feel hungover, or to try cutting alcohol out completely, this guide is unique in that it helps you define your goal.

There's an idea out there that you have to have a drinking problem, hit bottom, or declare yourself an alcoholic before making changes to your drinking habits - and once you do - the only option for you is total abstinence. What I've learned is that this simply isn't the case. As I mentioned earlier, a study by the CDC found that approximately 90% of excessive drinkers did not meet the criteria for alcohol dependence. This means that only about 10% of the people who use alcohol will go on to have a serious drinking problem. Unfortunately, though several studies have demonstrated that controlled drinking is possible and that moderation-based treatments may be preferred over abstinence-only approaches, the public and institutional views of alcohol treatment still support zero-tolerance, perpetuating the idea that "one drink makes a drunk."

Even though you may not be at risk for a long-term serious drinking problem, that doesn't mean that you are not allowed to make some changes. As I often discuss with my clients, you are the only one who gets to decide whether you want to make some changes to your drinking, based on how it makes you feel. You might hear things from friends and family members like "What? You don't have a drinking problem!!" because you might not fit society's portrayal of what a problem drinker "looks like".

More and more women are seeking to change their drinking habits, because they want to both feel better and be healthier. You don't need to wait until you spiral out of control or hit rock bottom before making some changes. In fact, your chances of learning to control your drinking by using the moderation techniques described in this book are much better the sooner you start.

But, if you are anything like I was, you might have an underlying fear that having less alcohol in your life will mean less fun. What I have learned over the years is that the opposite is true. By cutting back on alcohol you can experience more fun than you ever thought possible and get the most out of life- and this guide will show you how.

So take a moment and ask yourself the following:

Can you imagine waking up in the morning energized about your day, feeling clear and confident, without any gaps in the evening before, with only great memories and experiences?

Are you ready to finally be free of shame and regret, and to live a life that is fully, wholly and exquisitely you?

Are you ready to have more fun and adventure than you ever thought possible, without alcohol (or a lot less of it)?

Are you ready to finally plug that alcohol-induced hole in your wallet, once and for all?

Are you ready to have honest, fulfilling relationships with friends and lovers who respect and honour you?

Are you ready for something new and break the cycles you've been repeating over and over?

If you've said yes to any or all of these questions - this guide is for you.

HOW TO USE THIS GUIDE:

Chances are if you've picked up this guide, it's because you want to make some changes. Or you may have a feeling that this information will be helpful to someone with whom you are close. Either way, this guide is designed to provide small, actionable steps that you can begin to implement right away.

Throughout each chapter, I include real examples from friends and clients. Unfortunately, there is still a lot of stigma and shame around the issue of "drinking too much," even though it is something that so many of us do from time to time. That is why names and certain identifying features have been changed, except when I'm speaking about myself.

While these strategies have been tried and tested (with great success) by my clients, I also wanted to include the scientific evidence and research that explains how and why these strategies work. It is important for me that you know this is not a "juicy tell-all story" of my adventures in drinking and one woman's way out - all of the strategies are backed up by evidence as to why they actually work. For complete references of all of the studies included in this guide, please see the references section at the end.

Finally, each chapter concludes with actionable steps or activity: the root of both of those words being... to act! Unfortunately, you can't think or read your way into a new way of being. It's great that you decided to read this guide and get informed, but it's not enough to simply read the information.

Know that creating change takes consistent action and practice. It might feel weird or uncomfortable at first. I get it. It felt strange for me at first too. Don't get discouraged!

Remember to go easy on yourself. You are unlearning behaviours that were a lot of years in the making. The strategies in this guide are meant to build on one another. Try one or two, and then add another one in the next night.

If you "slip up," know that it's okay - it happens. Try not to beat yourself up if you feel you might have taken a step backwards. It's actually a very normal part of the process, and each moment is an opportunity to learn more about yourself.

Your success will be defined by you. Whether your goal is to never experience another blackout or hangover, have mind-blowing sober sex, have more energy in the mornings, learn how to add more fun and balance during the week so that you don't binge on the weekends, or cut alcohol out completely for a while - taking action on the steps in this guide will ensure your success.

Though it might be tempting to skip over the first couple of chapters to get to the "how-tos" of your big night out, please don't skim over them. The first three chapters are designed to create a foundation of information and support for your goals, on which the rest of the strategies build on.

Your first action steps?

1. Go and select a beautiful journal or diary to record your thoughts, reflections and action steps as you go through this guide.
2. Set aside some time every evening for the next ten days to read this guide.
3. Start to take action. By taking consistent action on the action steps included in this guide, you will have the tools and strategies to start making changes to your relationship to alcohol!

1

"I can't do this anymore" - Setting new intentions: visualizing a "new you"

"Intention is the starting point of every dream. It is the creative power that fulfills all of our needs."

— DEEPAK CHOPRA

You've picked up this guide for a reason. You want to drink less, while still having an incredible time. That's fantastic! I'm sure you are looking forward to learning how to do it, but first, you have to get clear on the "why." Step one starts with intentions.

Setting an intention is different than setting a goal. Your goal might be "I want to have a great time without blackouts" or "I want to cut out alcohol altogether for a while" or "I want to have fun while drinking no more than 3 drinks."

I used to think "Ugh, I never want to get drunk again," or "I am so over having killer hangovers," yet these statements did nothing to change my outcomes the next time around. I was stating goals without being clear on how I was going to achieve them, and without creating clear intentions.

Let's break down the dictionary definition of an intention. It has two parts: the aim or objective (which is the goal part) and the quality of the purposefulness. As with the examples above, you could be very clear on the first part but fall short in the second.

When the mind is not clear about the purpose, it tends to focus on what it doesn't want, rather than creating a clear picture of what it does want.

Let's take the statement 'I don't want to get drunk anymore' as an example. That's the goal, yet there's no clear picture of the purpose. The mind, filling in the blanks, will focus more on the word "drunk", because that's what it knows and has experience with. Without creating a clear intention or picture of what "not drunk" looks like for you, you are more likely to keep repeating the same pattern.

It's the same if you focus only on the number of drinks you want to drink (or not drink as the case may be), without digging deeper into why you want to cut back and how it will make you feel when you do so.

People without clear intentions can often roll aimlessly from one situation they don't want, to another, and ultimately they keep perpetuating a cycle of avoidance.

Have you ever thought to yourself "I don't want to get drunk... so I guess I shouldn't go out"? You end up avoiding the situation (i.e. party or bar) because you don't want to get drunk, so you are missing out entirely.

Jessica, a former client, explains how this was for her - "When I first was trying to cut back on the amount I was drinking, I didn't know how to set intentions. So instead, I just avoided going out. But then I started missing my friends, so I gave in and went out again, but with the same results as before."

By setting clear intentions, you can reset this pattern.

Our minds make no distinction between imagination and reality. This means we can have fun with our intentions and dream up the best possible scenario for ourselves. It isn't so much about how many drinks you will or won't drink, it's about how you want to feel, and what you want to embody.

"I hadn't really envisioned what drinking less was going to look like, which was part of the problem," Jessica continues. "When I was able to start seeing myself in similar situations, but behaving differently, and with different outcomes, things began to shift."

Danielle LaPorte, creator of The Desire Map, talks about how "the foundation of a good relationship with intentions and goals is keeping in mind that the primary aim of setting and working toward them is to feel the way you want to feel... The goal-setting itself has to feel the way you most want to feel. The journey is indeed the destination."

That is why it is so important to create a meaningful experience around setting and exploring your intentions.

In addition to knowing how you want to feel at the end of the night, it's also important to check in on your current mental and emotional state. Have you noticed that you can drink the same amount of alcohol on two different occasions, and have the alcohol affect you differently, based on how you were feeling on those two separate days? The following activity will help you check in with yourself about this before you get caught off guard.

ACTIVITY: SETTING INTENTIONS

We know that not all nights out are created equal. Too often we head out into the evening without giving much thought as to how we are feeling that day, to where we are going, and how we might feel when we are there.

For this exercise, take a few minutes to write down your desires for yourself during your evening. Create an ambiance that feels good (such as putting on music, lighting some candles), make this a beautiful experience instead of a chore.

1. Mindset:

The first step is to gain more awareness of how your mindset and the setting in which you are drinking can contribute to your experience around alcohol, your "desired outcome" and how messy or unmanageable the evening might become.

Check in with yourself before setting your intentions for the evening. Ask yourself:

- How am I doing today? Am I stressed, tired, happy, excited (or whatever)?
- How was the week so far?
- Has something been bothering me that I haven't had a chance to deal with yet (or that I've been avoiding dealing with?)
- How am I feeling about myself this week?
- How do I want to feel at the end of the night?

2. Setting:

Next, consider where it is that you are going.

- Is it an intimate setting with close friends, a work event with free flowing alcohol or a sweaty nightclub or … (there are infinite possibilities, these are just a few examples)
- Do I know everyone who will be there? Am I on good terms with everyone? Is it a loving, supportive environment, or competitive and catty?
- Is there a chance I may run into someone who triggers me to feel stressed, anxious or not great about myself?
- Who I am going out with? How much do they drink and do I have a tendency to get drunk when I'm with them? Are they "shots at the bar!" kinda people? What is the likelihood of drinks being bought for me?

3. Assess:

Reflecting on your answers to the questions above, assess the various possibilities for the evening. How will your mindset and the setting affect your drinking? Are there similar situations from the past from which you can learn?

From here, you will set your intentions.

I'll give you an example.

1. My mindset:

I've had a crazy week. I've been working extra hours trying to meet a deadline. I'm feeling a bit undervalued and that my work is going unnoticed. To top it off, one of my colleagues made an offhand comment about my performance on the last project proposal we put together, which made me feel that she was judging my competency. I'm tired, but I just want to blow off some steam and stop stressing about work.

2. The setting

Some friends have invited me over for drinks before going to a lounge and then out dancing. There's a good chance I'll see my colleagues and some of our investors at the lounge. The DJ at the club we are going to is friend's with my ex, and it's likely that my ex will be there with his new girlfriend.

3. My assessment

Whenever I get ready to go out at this particular friend's house, we usually end up pre-gaming with at least one bottle of champagne before going out. My colleagues often buy us drinks, and based on what happened last time, I was pretty drunk by the time I got to the club. Even though my ex and I are on good terms, I'm nervous about seeing him with his new girlfriend, and I don't want to do or say anything I'll regret.

Based on my assessment of the possible scenario, I'll set my intentions for the evening.

INTENTIONS

I love getting ready to go out at my friend's house, but this time I won't have any champagne. I'll set my intention around how many drinks to have at the lounge and the same for the club. (There will more strategies in Chapters 3, 4 and 5 that will support you to gracefully and discreetly stick to this plan. For now it's just really important to get clear on your intentions).

NOW, WRITE IT DOWN! BE SPECIFIC. IT DOESN'T HAVE TO TAKE LONG OR BE COMPLICATED.

HERE'S AN EXAMPLE:

7-8:30 pm - Teesha's house: snacks and fresh juices

9 - 11pm - Rodmay Lounge: 2 glasses (5oz each) of white wine (MAX)

12:30 am - Club 550: 1 cocktail

Feelings:

Desired Outcome:

The next step is to really allow yourself to feel the desired feelings that you have for yourself.

How do you want to feel in each of the scenarios for the evening? What qualities do you want to embody (i.e. confident, flirty, fun, open)?

Spend a few minutes sitting quietly, allowing yourself to imagine and visualize exactly how it will feel to be this version of you throughout the evening.

VISUALIZATION

Visualization is a practice that can help you mentally prepare and practice handling potentially stressful or challenging situations, and also practice the positive outcome that you are desiring.

I'm going to show you how to visualize in a way that is simple and easy and effective.

It is now an accepted practice for athletes to use visualization in preparation for a big event or game. I adapted the following steps from peak performance training that professional athletes use to prepare for a big game. They are designed to be simple, and this whole exercise is meant to be fun for you.

1) Begin every visualization with relaxation. Choose an environment that is quiet and free from distractions.

2) Have a specific intention for your visualization session - this is where you can bring in the elements of the intention you've set for the

desired outcome of your evening. We will talk later in this guide about specific strategies that will help this visualization become more realistic, but, for now, it's imperative to get clear on how you want to feel at the end of the evening and bring this intention to your visualization.

3) Play out your whole evening in your mind as you are want to experience it. It is not about just "seeing" or picturing in your mind's eye, but hearing, smelling, and, most important, feeling as you would if you were actually in that situation. Mentally create, in as much vivid detail as possible (i.e. seeing, hearing, feeling, etc.) your event, party, or whatever scenario you are planning which involves alcohol.

As with any skill, visualization takes practice - Be persistent when you practice and keep at it. With daily repeated practice, you will improve your ability to "see," "feel" and "hear" the "new you" into being.

This visualization process isn't meant to be long, in fact, a shorter session, between 5-10 minutes but repeated frequently, can be very useful.

The key here is to start bringing intention to your evening. Doing this will help avoid those situations where you wake up the next day wondering how you ended up getting so drunk or trying to piece together the details.

As one of my clients said - "I felt awkward writing everything down at first, but then I became so clear on what I wanted and how to do it. Once I got clear on my intentions, everything shifted."

In the next chapter, we will go into more specific detail about how setting clear intentions and using visualization can help create the positive mindset needed to achieve the change you are desiring.

ACTION STEPS:

1. Review the Mindset activity and practice with a few real life scenarios (as in - situations you've been in or know you will be in soon).
2. Pick an upcoming scenario that you might find yourself in and spend 5-10 minutes practicing the visualization exercise to explore the new outcome you'd like for yourself.

"Our intention creates our reality."

— Dr. Wayne Dyer

2

"But what if I can't change?" The Power of Positive Thinking: Building the belief that change IS possible for you

"You are the sum total of everything you've ever seen, heard, eaten, smelled, been told, forgot - it's all there. Everything influences each of us, and be- cause of that I try to make sure that my experiences are positive."

- MAYA ANGELOU

Now that you've become clear on your intentions, it is time to set yourself up for success. Before we continue, I want to acknowledge that the very fact that you are willing to look at your drinking habits and set some new intentions is worth celebrating! You've taken a big step in a new direction, and that takes a lot of courage.

Now for some tough love. You can have the clearest intentions in the world but if you don't believe you are capable of changing, they won't do you much good.

You might be eager to jump right into the strategies to have you drinking less while having a great night out but stick with me, please. What I've learned from years of personal experience (hello trial and error) is that you can have all in the information in the world, but if you aren't clear on your intentions and aren't in the right mindset, it will be a lot harder to change your behaviour.

Even after I became clear on my intentions to drink less, I felt like I was in a negative feedback loop, inevitably repeating the same pattern, despite my best intentions.

After going through an especially heart-breaking time, I found myself drinking way more than I wanted to (yet again). What seemed like a harmless dinner out with girlfriends ended with me doing cocaine in a stairwell in an ally (classy, I know) and led to one of the worst hangovers of my life. It is hard for me to admit, even now. This happened during my training to become a holistic health coach, and after I had already decided that I wanted to focus on helping women who struggle with alcohol.

There I was, "messing up," again. This is what the voice in my head told me: "You aren't capable of change, who do you to think you are, you're a fraud!"

I realized I was missing a crucial piece. I had set my intentions, but I didn't quite believe that I was capable of sticking to them. I didn't believe that another way was possible for me. Going even deeper, I didn't believe I was worthy of the change that I wanted to make. The practices described in this chapter helped me finally break free of the negative cycle and shame spiral into which I found myself repeatedly falling.

Shame is a deep feeling of inadequacy, inferiority, or self-loathing. It can make you want to hide or disappear. It can also cause a deep, desperate feeling of separation from those around you. No matter how much love you are surrounded by, you might feel completely alone.

Shame can stem from early childhood experiences,
starting as early as infancy. Experiences of shame
often lead us to self-beliefs such as:
I'm unworthy (of love)
I'm no good
I'm a failure
I'm unlovable
I don't deserve happiness
I'm defective (i.e., there's something inherently wrong with me)
I'm a fraud (i.e. I'm just really good at pretending to be likable/
successful... somehow I've managed to fool everyone around me!)

It's no surprise that when you experience deep shame you may turn to alcohol, drugs or other substances to "fill the hole." And also for connection; an attempt to fix the isolation these shameful feelings can cause. Or on the flip side, you might do or say things while under the influence that then trigger deep pre-existing feelings of shame, which layers shame upon more shame, and which I call the Shame Spiral.

Brene Brown, whose research and stories have had a profound impact on me, writes in her book "I thought it was just me: Women reclaiming power and courage in a culture of shame", "Shame corrodes the very part of us that believes we are capable of change."

When my clients first come to me, they are also often feeling pretty hopeless. They want so desperately for things to be different, but after years of having the same outcome, they are starting to feel like they will never change. This is a dangerous place to be. The more a person begins to believe that they cannot change, the more likely they are to keep repeating the same pattern of drunkenness, blackouts and out of control behavior.

After an unexpectedly drunk night, in which she fell and twisted her ankle, Claire, a 37-year-old client who is the president of a new tech firm, lamented to me "I just feel like I'm doomed to keep doing the same s**t over and over. I'm tired of it." Jackie, another client in her early 40s, wrote to me in a moment of desperation saying, "It's hard to believe that I'm not going to end up like my mother."

And Sandra, though younger than the other two in so far as her history with drinking, kept dwelling on all of the mistakes she had made in the past, beating herself up for all of her "stupid" mistakes while drinking too much.

Our minds are very powerful. If Claire believes and keeps repeating to herself that she is doomed and will never change, and if Jackie is convinced she is going to end up like her mother, and if Sandra keeps dwelling on the fact that she's stupid and is going to keep making mistakes, the odds are that is the reality in which they are going to find themselves.

For that reason, it is important that we take a moment to talk about the power of positive thinking.

Dr Masaru Emoto, a researcher and alternative healer from Japan, demonstrated the power of positive thinking in what has come to be known as the "rice experiment." As reported in an article in yoganonymous.com, Dr Emoto placed portions of cooked rice into two containers. On one container he wrote "thank you" and on the other "you fool". He then instructed school children to say the labels on the jars out loud everyday when they passed them by. After 30 days, the rice in the container with positive thoughts had barely changed, while the other was moldy and rotten.

"Even our worst enemies don't talk about us the way we talk to ourselves."

- ARIANNA HUFFINGTON

As we now know from Chapter 1, we attract or draw to ourselves what we dwell on. Time to "flip the switch" so to speak.

You can dwell on the bad, or you can look for the good. I remember when I was going through a particularly rough time a couple of years ago, my coach Kristen Domingue, said to me: "Caitlin, never forget - the Universe never gives you more than you can handle. You got this."

You got this too! I've seen countless women change their drinking patterns by learning to set intentions, thinking differently about themselves and their relationship to alcohol, and implementing the strategies we will get into in a bit more detail later in this guide.

The following is an activity that I recommend to all of my one-to-one coaching clients, called the Thrive Threesome. The teachings of several important mentors weave together to create the components of this practice: three things you can do daily to help you thrive and flip the script in your head from negative self-talk to empowered belief in your capacity to change.

I remember when Tessa started working with me, she was always beating herself up, about everything. It seemed at times that she didn't believe that change was possible... similarly to Claire, who felt she was doomed to keep repeating the same pattern. She started writing her Thrive Threesome daily. On our next call, which was two weeks later, she said she already noticed a significant shift in how she was thinking about herself.

I suggest doing this every day. Some people prefer to do it before bed, others when they wake up in the morning. Experiment with what feels best to you. The key is to try to build it into your routine and do it consistently.

However, if you are reading this right before getting ready for a big night out, and you haven't had a chance to include this in your daily routine, no worries. Spend a few minutes on this after setting your intentions and before getting ready to go out.

GRATITUDE

The first piece is gratitude. I'm sure you've heard it before, but the importance of creating a daily practice of gratitude cannot be overstated. Gabrielle Bernstein, best-selling author of "Spirit Junkie" and "May Cause Miracles", talks about using gratitude to "find your way back to yourself," and to your true center, which is love. When described this way, you can see how important gratitude can be to counteract the negative voices in our head. When we are grateful for what we have, we create more energy around the good in our life and attract more of that good to us.

If this still sounds a little "airy-fairy" as my grandmother would say, I've included some research to back it up. Martin Seligman, Robert Emmons, and Michael McCullough are three scientists who have focused on the study of gratitude and its relationship to health and mental well-being. They've found that people who keep gratitude journals on a weekly basis have been found to exercise more regularly, have fewer physical ailments, feel better about their lives as a whole, and feel more optimistic about their upcoming week. They've also found that daily discussions of gratitude results in higher reported levels of alertness, enthusiasm, determination, attentiveness, energy, and sleep duration and quality. Grateful people also report lower levels of depression and stress, although they do not deny or ignore the negative aspects of life.

Though the importance of practicing gratitude can not be overstated, I understand that it can sometimes be difficult to find something for which to be grateful. Start with locating qualities within yourself that you always know to be true and give thanks or self-appreciation. I've given some examples in the activity section at the end of this chapter.

DESIRE

The second component of the Thrive Threesome is the concept of desire. Dara McKinley, the creator of the Goddess Process, teaches that our power as women lies in our ability to connect with and express our desires. I have to admit, when I was first introduced to this concept, I was like "say what!?! Desires? I'm allowed to have those!?!" Maybe you are thinking the same thing!

A few years ago, I was fortunate to be a guest teacher at a series of retreats that Dara organized in Mexico, which was a profound and transformational experience for me. It was there that I started understanding the power of my desire. I learned how creating a daily practice around my desires could ultimately break me out of the negative feedback loop in my head and the voices that told me I was unworthy and unable to change.

Dara also introduced me to the teachings of Regena Thomashauer, more commonly known now as Mama Gena, who is a pioneer in researching the nature of pleasure. She has dedicated her life to the discipline of pleasure and fun. Though focusing on pleasure might seem superficial, her work is actually deeply profound.

"A desire is anything but frivolous. It is the interface between you and that which is greater than you. No desire is meaningless or inconsequential. If it pulls you, even a little bit, it will take everyone higher. Desire is where the Divine lives, inside the inspiration of your desire. Every desire is of profound importance with huge consequences, and deserves your attention."

- MAMA GENA

Shortly after that, I became acquainted with work of Danielle LaPorte. I consider Danielle a mentor whom I've never actually met in person. She is so committed to the importance desire plays in our lives that she created "The Desire Map", a program to be guided by our inner feelings and desires.

BRAGS

The third, but no less important component of the Thrive Threesome, is to brag. Might sound strange, especially because as women we are often taught not to be vocal about our successes. However, bragging is essential to help us locate and celebrate the greatness within us.

By doing a daily practice of bragging, you are celebrating what you have already succeeded in - you are making your greatness visible to yourself. In her book "The School of the Womanly Arts", Mama Gena dedicates a whole chapter to the importance of bragging to celebrate the good in your life and unearth your desires. In one of her blogs, Danielle LaPorte shared that reminding yourself of your previous successes keeps you grounded in what is real and possible in terms of change.

You see how powerful of a practice the Thrive Threesome can be in creating the positive mindset for success. But don't take my word for it - try it yourself!

ACTION STEPS:

1. Find a consistent time each day to write in your journal.
2. Write a minimum of 3 for each of the Thrive Threesomes:

   Gratitudes/Self-Appreciations (locate the qualities inside of yourself you want to focus on, honour what already exists, call in more good)

   Desires (what do you want for yourself? This can be anything you hope, dream or wish for - try not to censor yourself. Examples of mine include: I desire fulfilling and meaningful work, I desire a strong body, I desire more respectful and skilled dance partners, I desire trusting relationships, I desire more play, I desire less pressure on myself etc.

   Brags (evidence of your successes, things you are awesome at, when things have gone right for you)

   Review your intentions from the previous Chapter, and now you have given yourself a powerful dose of positivity and are already stepping into your evening equipped with the best mindfulness juju you can give yourself.

   If you need some extra oompf before heading out in the evening; if you are feeling anxious, nervous or stressed; or your negative self-talk is a little too loud - consider doing all of this as part of your "getting ready" activities.

Every day brings new choices.

MARTHA BECK

3

"What if I mess up?" Creating Accountability Strategies to support you as you change

"Accountability separates the wishers in life from the action takers that

care enough about their future to account for their daily actions."

- JOHN DI LEMME

Intentions, Mindset and Accountability are the three pillars of your "Drink Less Success." These three are the foundation that the upcoming strategies build upon. Without putting time and effort into building a solid foundation, the strategies will be shaky, and more likely to fall through.

What exactly does accountability mean?

Accountability, simply put, is both the ability and willingness to take responsibility for one's actions. It is easy to live our lives blaming others for our downfall but willingly taking responsibility shifts you from being the victim of circumstance to being the empowered leader of your life.

Todd Herman, a business management consultant and trainer for high-performance athletes, defines personal accountability as "being willing to answer ... for the outcomes resulting from your choices, behaviors, and actions."

Any of these sound familiar?

"My friends kept buying me drinks."

"The bartender was pouring my drinks too strong."

"It was an open bar!! I can't say no to free alcohol!"

"One word: Shots."

Those are all examples of being unwilling to accept personal responsibility for your actions, and blaming your issues on external factors.

Want to make some changes? Hint - stop blaming, and start being accountable.

One of my favourite slogans from the Al-Anon meetings I've attended is: "Let it begin with me." It is so easy for us to externalize our problems and our patterns. However, when it comes down to it, if we find ourselves stuck in the same pattern, we have no one to blame but ourselves. Taking action on the content in Chapters 1 and 2 is so important to your Drink Less Be More success for this reason. Do the work, get clear on your intentions, and make a daily practice of your Thrive Threesome.

Taking responsibility for your actions does not mean that you must do this all on your own. To the contrary, being accountable can include enlisting a support team, which is sometimes a crucial element of taking action.

When I ask my clients why they decided to hire a coach, one of the main reasons they state is accountability. It's the knowing that they have another person on their team to help them stay true to the intentions they've set for themselves. My clients recognize that simply thinking about, or talking about, wanting to make a change usually isn't enough.

Have you noticed that some people have a very good internal accountability monitor? They are really good at following through on the goals they set for themselves, while many of us (probably the majority reading this guide) function better when we outsource accountability? There is a reason run clubs are popular! There may be a few people who can get up at the crack of dawn by their gumption - but many of us need our group or run buddy cheering us out of bed. If you are someone who procrastinates, works better with external deadlines, and naturally finds yourself asking friends or your partner to remind you of certain things, then finding an accountability partner is probably a good option for you.

Your accountability strategy does not have to include paid support though it is an option to consider. You may want to enlist a loved one, family member or friend to help you with your accountability. Chapter 7 will go more in depth into our close relationships, and how to talk to people you love about the changes you want to make. For now, it's really important to have someone "on your team" as you plan a big night out or are getting ready for a special event. You can also look to see what kind of support programs or groups exist in your community or online. There are plenty of sober resources; however resources to drink less or in moderation are more limited. I've included a list of recommended online groups to check out at the end of this chapter.

SIP SISTERS

Long before I even knew what a health coach was, let alone began studying to be one, I found a friend who became my accountability buddy in redefining my relationship to alcohol. We created a shared google document and used it to write our intentions, be honest about our challenges, and seek support from one another. We called each other "sip sisters." Our goal wasn't a lifetime of sobriety, though we both tried and appreciated periods of sobriety. Our goal was to learn how to drink in moderation, having a great time without going overboard. Learning how to "sip" seemed like a good metaphor for drinking in moderation; it denotes the ability to slowly savour and enjoy rather than suck back drinks like there's no tomorrow.

Here are some of the qualities you will want to look for in a Sip Sister (accountability buddy):

Non-judgemental - Look for someone who can be empathetic, understanding and caring. This one might seem like a no-brainer, but what does non-judgemental mean to you? For example, if you have different goals, one person simply wanting to drink less, and the other trying to be sober, it might be difficult to understand the other person's choices.

Shared experiences and goals - It will help your Sip Sister to be empathic and understanding if you have similar experiences and goals in mind. Finding someone who also wants to explore the "Drink Less Be More" philosophy is a good starting place.

Firm but loving - Sip Sisters are honest and direct in their feedback and observations, and loving in their delivery. You know that you can count on them to "tell it like it is" while doing their best to show you that no matter what you are loved and supported.

Responsible and resourceful - Your Sip Sister should be good at keeping commitments, showing up for scheduled check ins, sending you texts and reminders when you need it, etc. It is also a great help if your accountability buddy helps you find new solutions if you find yourself slipping or repeating the same patterns.

A little while ago in our private online support group, an internet friend of mine wrote that she wanted to take 30 days off alcohol, and asked if anyone wanted to join her. I had been drinking a bit more regularly than I wanted to, and a bit more than I wanted to each time, so I decided to hit the reset button with her.

The thing is, I didn't tell anyone in my "real life" what I was doing. So when the time came to have a glass of wine poured at dinner, nothing was stopping me from saying yes. I felt bashful the next day when it came time to check in with my internet buddy who had initiated the challenge. But when it came time to come clean about the night before, she divulged that she had had an even wilder night that night with her boyfriend who works in the bar industry!

At first glance, it might seem like this was a failed experiment in accountability. What good is an online accountability if we both just continued business as usual and didn't stick to our intentions?

Let me describe what happened next. After sharing our initial slip-ups with each other, we regrouped and supported each other to figure out where we got derailed. Turns out that neither of us had communicated our intentions with our significant others - so how could we expect them to support us? We also didn't have explicit alternate strategies in place (more on this in the next two chapters). So we recommitted to our goals, with renewed energy and support from each other, and strategies that would address the particular challenges that might come up given each of our individual situations.

If I hadn't believed that this Sip Sister was non-judgemental, I may never have totally opened up to her, therefore limiting my ability to go deeper into strategizing and finding solutions that would work. We had similar experiences, goals, and desires, we were firm and loving with each other, and we helped each other brainstorm next-level strategies that would work.

OTHER ACCOUNTABILITY STRATEGIES

Gretchen Rubin, self-professed happiness expert and author of many books on the topic, describes habits as the invisible architecture of everyday life, and a significant element of happiness. In her book, "Better than Before", she describes the strategies we can exploit to change our habits, including... you guessed it - accountability!

Gretchen also explains that not everyone will respond to the same kind of accountability because some people are more responsive to private accountability, and some of us respond better to public accountability.

I am definitely a public accountability kind of gal - an example of this is declaring certain intentions on Facebook or in certain group forums for school. However, I appreciate a mix of public and private because there are certain details I prefer to keep to myself or between a small, select group. You will find the combination of accountability strategies that works before for you - the key, as always, is to put them in place and take action on them.

SET REMINDERS

Technology can be your best friend at times. I love setting reminders in my phone that give me a boost during the day or night. If I feel like I'm heading into a situation that might be particularly challenging, I set a reminder for myself with words of encouragement. We'll dive deeper into this in Chapter 5 when we talk strategies, but it's a good idea to start putting this into practice now.

Alternatively, if you'd prefer to take a techno-break, consider a good luck charm or amulet. It can be in the form of a bracelet, ring or another accessory that you can easily see. Write down your intentions in your journal, and state clearly of what the charm will remind you. Then, every time you see the charm, you will be reminded of your intentions for yourself.

GIVE YOURSELF A REWARD

How will you feel after a month of sticking to your Drink Less Be More intentions? Pretty great, right? And think about all that money you will have saved from spending less money on drinks every week.

Consider setting a monthly or even weekly reward for yourself as an incentive to stick with your intentions. How about a massage, spa date, concert, or weekend getaway? After a month of sticking to your intentions, you will deserve it!

START A SIP SISTER PLAY GROUP

I read somewhere that you are the sum of the five people with whom you spend the most time. Understandably, not all of your friends might be on board with your new intentions for moderate drinking. However, there may be more people than you think in your life who are willing to give it a try.

Consider starting a study group to review the chapters in the book, and help each other stay accountable and on track with your intentions. This group could be online (Facebook groups are great for this, and you can set the privacy setting to "secret" if you want to keep it confidential), or in person.

I have a dream that someday soon there can be Sip Sister meet-ups in every city!

HOST A DRINK LESS BE MORE MEETUP

If you are a public accountability kinda gal, be bold! Make your intentions public by announcing your desire to drink less and start getting the most out of life! Set up an event, be clear about your intentions in the event invite, and ask others to join in.

ACTION STEPS:

Let's recap the first three chapters.

1. What is your current intention to drink less? Get inside the feeling, and understand the "why." Try setting aside 30 minutes at the beginning of each week to journal on this topic.

2. Positive Mindset - are you feeling confident in your ability to stick to your intentions? Have you been practicing the Thrive Threesome? If not, take the time to write in your journal now. Set your alarm 10 minutes earlier or set aside 10 minutes each day to practice your Thrive Threesome.

3. List three accountability strategies your are going to try for the next two weeks. Describe these strategies in as much detail as possible, and don't forget to schedule them! If your strategy involves reaching out to someone else, do that now. Remember, as my business mentor Marie Forleo always says, "If it's not scheduled, it's not real" - so make sure to actually put these time slots into your calendar. Do it now!

"If you hang out with chickens, you're going to cluck and if you hang out with eagles, you're going to fly."

—Steve Maraboli

4

"Can I still have fun getting ready?" Getting Ready: New pre-gaming strategies

"Elegance is not the prerogative of those who have just es-caped from ado- lescence, but of those who have already taken possession of their future."

- COCO CHANEL

Now that we've covered the foundational pillars of your new relationship with alcohol, you can begin creating new habits for yourself. What you do before leaving the house can have as much impact on the outcome of your evening as how many drinks you drink during your night.

GETTING READY

Changing your "pre-gaming" activities can help set the tone for the evening, and help ensure that you are starting off on the right foot, so to speak.

The more you pay attention and set your intentions, the less likely you are to end up having one of those "I don't know what happened" kind of nights.

EAT SOMETHING!

This may seem obvious, but having food in your stomach slows the absorption of alcohol into your bloodstream and will help delay the effects of alcohol, which will help you stick to your intentions.

The thing is, many of us women tend to not want to eat that much before going out, preferring to nibble on a salad or some veggies... then wonder why we're ravenously hungry and ready to inhale an entire pizza and cheesy fries at 3am. This tendency to eat less before going out is one of the reasons why alcohol can affect women more quickly. If you skip dinner, alcohol will enter your bloodstream faster, and your blood alcohol content will rise more rapidly. If you are trying to get drunk fast, this is one way to do it! Eating before you go out is an important strategy to follow, as it will cause alcohol to drip into your body's system, rather than flooding it.

Proteins and fats take longer to digest, so they'll stay in your system longer into the evening. Try eating a meal with healthy fats such as avocado, salmon, chia, olive or coconut oil, as fats take the longest to digest and will stay in your stomach longer. Even if you think there will be food at the event you are heading to - it's a good idea to start the night off with a snack, or a meal. Eating first will help maintain your energy level through the evening. This is important if you don't want to feel like you are "crashing" - because, let's face it - you are then more likely to want a drink as a pick me up!

PRE-DRINKING

My best friend and I used to polish off a bottle of champagne before heading out to the first venue of the evening. We loved getting ready together, finding outfits, doing our hair and makeup, listening to music, all the while sipping liquid happiness. Drinking bubbly felt like a treat, a celebration, and that's often exactly the feeling we were going for, as we sought to shed the stress of the week.

This was a hard habit to break... but when we both committed to controlling our drinking, our pre-game strategy had to change. We were still fans of the bubbly, so we sought out non-alcoholic versions. Many of my clients have commented on how the one act of changing what they drink at the end of a long day, or before getting ready to go out, has dramatically changed their outcome on the evening.

Check out your local specialty health food store for healthy and organic bubblies that are low on sugar and artificial sweeteners/ingredients. Sparkling apple cider (dry) and elderflower sparkling water were two favorites of mine. Try making your own concoctions by adding frozen fruit, fresh fruit juices, ginger, lemon/lime or mint to sparkling water. Get creative! The trick is to still be celebratory and treat yourself in the taste department.

These non-alcoholic beverages are also great for bringing to dinner parties, BBQs, picnics or any social BYOB-type event. The key is to make sure you feel like you are treating yourself, not depriving yourself, when you cut back on alcohol.

A helpful reminder is also the number of empty calories you are cutting back on by eliminating the boozy drinks before the bar. With each sip of your savoury elixir, remind yourself of the commitment you've made to your happiness, health, and wellbeing.

NEW RITUALS

Now, instead of knocking back half a bottle or more of booze before even leaving the house, I have created new rituals for myself. I spend a few moments meditating on my intentions and celebrating the path that I am on, living my most beautiful and radiant self. I put on my favourite "getting ready like a goddess" playlist - songs that make me feel sexy and have me dancing around the room as I pick out my outfit. I always have the ingredients for yummy elixirs readily available, and I make sure to include a meal or at least a hefty snack in my pre-party plans.

Of course, it really helps to have friends who are on board with you. I remember shortly after I'd committed to not drinking so much, I was invited to an early evening event at a friend's house. There were bottles of champagne, and it was so tempting to pour myself glass after glass. Thankfully, I had already chatted with her about my intentions and she also had some non-alcoholic bubbly and fresh juices. For more in-depth accountability strategies, don't forget to review Chapter 3, and upcoming Chapter 7 will give you more ideas about what to say to friends to get them on board.

ENLIST YOUR SMARTPHONE

Put that accessory to good use! While planning your evening, use your phone to create little reminders that will help you stay on track. Think of them like little mini-affirmations sprinkled through your evening. Time them as alerts, alarms or reminders to pop up at crucial moments throughout the evening.

Example:
10:00 - Hey beautiful. Don't forget to drink water to keep a clear mind!
11:30 - You are sexier when you're sober!! You got this!
12:00 - Hey yo cinderella. Why don't you take yourself home, before you turn into a pumpkin?

You might remember Sandra from Chapter 2, who used to be really good at talking herself out of things. She began implementing this technique and describes the power of these thoughtfully timed reminders, "Just as I was starting to talk myself out of my intentions, the reminders helped me stay on track."

ACTION STEPS

Login to the members website, browse the tasty, alcohol-free drinks recipes and pick one that you are going to try. Make sure to have the ingredients ready in your house, so you aren't left scrambling when it comes time to pour yourself a drink.

1. What are some new rituals you can create to enhance your evening - to help you connect with and radiate the beautiful goddess that you are, inside and out? List them in your journal.
2. Create a pre-party playlist focusing on making you feel great, confident, sexy and grounded.
3. Set your reminders in your phone.

5

"How will I do things differently?"
Same Party, Different You

"First you take a drink, then the drink takes a drink, then the drink takes you."

— F. Scott Fitzgerald

Finally!! The strategies you've been waiting for. Now that you are out of the house - it is going to be even more important to stick to your intentions. These sure-fire tips and tricks will help you sail gracefully through your evening and make it home with your memories intact.

HOLD UP!
Strategy #1 is... do nothing!! Yes, it sounds strange, I know, so let's discuss. Think about how much we do on autopilot, without really thinking about it. How many times have you sat down at a restaurant table, and immediately began perusing the wine list? Or ordered a cocktail while waiting for your party to arrive? Or grabbed that glass of champagne off the server's tray of drinks at a networking event? Or arrived at the club, bee-lined for the bar, and ordered your favourite drink before you even registered what song is playing? My guess is that you can say yes to all of these questions - and you aren't alone.

To combat this automated response, I like to implement the "arrive and assess" strategy. Give yourself 30 minutes after arriving somewhere to check in with yourself, see how you feel, and try something different. This simple step with help you reset your evening in a big way.

At a restaurant? Ask what kind of delicious non-alcoholic offerings there are on the menu. You might be surprised! For so long I was only focused on the boozy section that I had no idea how many other tasty options there were. This strategy will also really help you to hold off on the alcohol until you have something in your stomach.

Arriving at a bar or club? Try a sparkling water with a splash of fruit and a lime wedge. Set the timer for 30 minutes before you order your first cocktail, and then follow the 2x1 strategy below.

BYO(NA)B

The NA means non-alcoholic of course, and the B is for Beverage, not Booze! This strategy obviously isn't meant for a night out on the town, but can work wonders in any sort of communal gathering such as a picnic, BBQ, dinner party, house party or any sort of communal gathering.

DRINK WATER

Alcohol is a diuretic, which means it makes you pee more, which can lead to dehydration. Not only does this lead to hangovers, but a dehydrated brain doesn't function as well, which will compound how you feel the effects of alcohol. Water is your friend - for so many reasons!

You needn't make your water drinking obvious - you can ask the bartender for sparkling or still water over ice with a few slices of lime or lemon. Drinking out of fancy glassware makes drinking water more appealing and more delicious in my experience. It also cuts down on public scrutiny, judgement, and having to answer unsolicited questions about why you aren't drinking alcohol.

A few years ago my friend Valeria was trying to cut down on drinking. She was the consummate party persona, and when she showed up at the bar, everyone expected her to have on her party hat. She complained to me that her friends continued to pressure her to drink and that she felt uncomfortably conspicuous when she wasn't drinking alcohol. I asked her what she was drinking, and she said bottled water!

By drinking water out of the bottle, she immediately stood out as "not drinking," which was out of character and, of course, prompted a lot of questions and pressure. I suggested that she try drinking sparkling water with a splash of cranberry and a lime wedge and asked her to report back. Not surprisingly, the night time she went out hardly anyone noticed she wasn't drinking alcohol, and she didn't feel like a "loser" (her words not mine)!

TWO-TO-ONE...

You may have heard the one-for-one rule: alternating every alcoholic beverage with a glass of water, hence one for one. It has been my experience, and that of many friends and clients of mine, that this is not enough water (or time!) between drinks. It's still possible to pound your way through a glass of water, and then an alcoholic beverage, then another glass of water, then another alcoholic beverage in less than an hour. If you do, you are still consuming alcohol at a faster rate and a larger quantity than you should be if trying to cut back. While drinking plenty of water can slow the uptake of alcohol into your bloodstream, it will not dilute the amount of alcohol you are drinking. More water does not equal permission to drink more alcohol.

Challenge yourself with a two-to-one ratio. Sip two non-alcoholic drinks (at least!) to every alcoholic beverage. If you want more variety, try alternating one glass of still or sparkling water with lemon and one mocktail. Your skin, your waistline and your brain cells will thank you for it! Plus, it's great way to spread your drinks out, and more easily stick to your intentions.

ASK THE BARTENDER

Get fancy! Cutting back on alcohol doesn't have to be boring. To the contrary, there are infinite possibilities for your tasting pleasure. One of my favourite things to do is to ask the bartender to concoct the most delicious creation sans-alcohol that he or she can come up with. Any good mixologist will love the challenge. Request all-natural ingredients and low-sugar. Switch it up and try a savoury drink. Many bars now stock ingredients such as cucumber, basil, ginger, chillies, celery or vegetable juices, as well as infused natural syrups and fresh fruit.

Another way to enlist the bartender is by asking him or her to make you non-alcoholic drinks on the sly. If you are at a work or social event where you feel the pressure to drink, you can ask the bartender to make sure that when your colleague or client is ordering rounds of drinks, yours is made without alcohol. Make sure to tip them extra in appreciation for going the extra distance for you.

CHOOSE WISELY

Again, refer back to your intentions for the evening. If you've set a 3 drink limit for yourself, you are going to guzzle that amount pretty quickly if doing shots or ordering doubles. Whatever your magic number is for the night, I recommend the following golden rule to anyone looking to cut back on their alcohol for the evening while having a graceful and glorious night out:

No shots, no doubles (or triples) and no sugary drinks, which can cause your blood sugar to spike, and inevitably crash again (this includes sodas, artificial fruit juices, commercial syrups etc). Follow this golden rule and you are guaranteed more fun. Trust me on this one.

If you plan to have more than one or two drinks, follow Dr Oz's recommendations by choosing a lighter coloured liquid like vodka or gin. According to him, consuming large amounts of darker pours like whiskey and brandy can increase the severity of hangovers because dark drinks have higher concentrations of congeners, toxic compounds formed when alcohol is fermented.

DRINK SLOWLY

Sip your drinks. You are beautiful, confident and classy. If you are thirsty from shaking your beautiful booty - drink more water. Pick the slowest drinker in the group and pace yourself with her. I remember before I started trying to cut back on my alcohol intake, I couldn't believe how "slow" some people drank. Not surprisingly, it was the slow drinkers that still had their "ish" together at the end of the night. When I started pacing myself more leisurely, and really savouring my drinks, sipping and enjoying, I realized it's true, slow and steady does win the race.

ACT AS IF

The first few times you go out with your new intentions to drink less may feel strange and uncomfortable, particularly if you've been using alcohol to help you be more extroverted. A technique that helps is "acting as if." Imagine how you want to feel, the qualities you want to embody (refer to Chapter 1 if you need a reminder) and then fake it till you make it, as they say.

As Terri Cole, a well-respected psychotherapist and coach writes, "Any successful person will tell you that there was a time when they were filled with self-doubt, but many learned quickly to act "as if" they felt confident. This is not being dishonest or being in denial... Try on feeling confident until it fits, until it becomes who you are."

I realized I was getting really good at acting "as if" when I was out at a party with my sister a few years ago. I had been dancing around all night, having perfected my drunk-dancing so well that my sister's then-boyfriend was concerned when I was about to get in the car and drive. He was incredulous that the drink I'd had in my hand all night was orange juice and club soda!

BRUSH UP ON YOUR ONE-LINERS

Knowing what to say to the people who make your choice to drink less their business (even though it's not) can help you stick to your intentions. Having a one-liner ready and knowing in advance what to say to deflect their attention will help you feel confident and prepared.

One of the easiest answers to the question "why aren't you drinking?" or "would you like another drink?" is quite simply, "thank you, I'm great for right now." If pressed, you can say that you are on a cleanse, or cutting back for health reasons. It is generally quite difficult to argue with someone who is making choices for perceived medical or health-related reasons. I discuss the topic of what to say to acquaintances and loved ones in much more detail in Chapter 7.

KNOWING WHEN "ENOUGH IS ENOUGH"

It's a skill that many of us are not taught... to the contrary, in our culture of excess we often feel like we need more, more, more! Setting your intentions before you go out can help with your internal barometer of when enough is enough. The more clear you can become on what your desired outcome and feeling is, the more you'll know if you've achieved it, and if you are not going to, then when to call it quits.

Carissa is a good example of this. A successful personal trainer and coach in New York, she was used to pushing through her exhaustion and introversion by drinking excessively and then staying out way later than she planned. When she learned to moderate her alcohol, she could more easily stick to her intention of going out, letting loose, having a great time and still getting home early enough to give her body the rest that it truly needed to keep up with the demands of her work and busy life.

HOME SWEET HOME

It can be tempting to pour yourself another glass when you get home, yet that nightcap can be the tipping point to a killer hangover the next day, and a guarantee of a less quality sleep. It is important to learn how to wind down at the end of the evening without drinking more. Bubble baths, calming aromatherapy diffusers, and aromatic teas are all great ways to wind down. If your stomach is feeling upset because of your drinking, try adding rosemary or lavender to your sleepy time tea. It can help to settle your stomach and have a calming effect to soothe you to sleep.

Keep your fridge stocked with coconut water or DIY electrolyte drinks or add a pinch of sea salt to a pint of water. Alcohol switches off an antidiuretic hormone, which is why you find you start peeing a lot during a night out. The constant trips to the bathroom deplete your body's level of salt, so that glass of slightly salted water will start to put things straight.

GET YOUR BEAUTY SLEEEEEEP

Our bodies need about an hour to metabolize alcohol, so avoiding a drink right before bed will also help you have a better night's sleep. It may feel like alcohol helps you sleep, which in a sense it does because the effects depress your central nervous system and you skip rapid eye movement (REM) sleep and go right into a deep sleep. However, as the effects of alcohol wear off you will be more likely to wake and sleep fitfully. In Dr Oz's guide to healthy drinking he recommends "Don't have a nightcap," stating that a 2013 analysis of more than 30 studies found that consuming two or more drinks less than two hours before bed decreased the amount of REM sleep.

During a regular night of sleep, you will usually go through 5-6 sleep cycles and will wake up feeling refreshed, but after a night of drinking you will likely only have 1-2 cycles and will wake up exhausted. Even if you think you are getting the recommended hours of sleep, drinking heavily the night before has been shown to exacerbate daytime sleepiness. All the more incentive to stick to your intentions and use your time before bed to hydrate and replenish.

Decide which of these strategies you are going to try. It helps to have a clear plan of which one(s) you will use before heading out for the evening. Deciding in advance allows you to be more in control of your outcomes, and will prevent the likelihood of "drawing a blank" when it comes time to order a drink at the bar, or falling back into familiar habits.

Let your sip sister, accountability buddy, or significant other know what your intentions and strategies are and let them know how they can best support you to stay on track.

> "I always did something I was a little not ready to do. I think that's how you grow. When there's that moment of 'Wow, I'm not really sure I can do this,' and you push through those moments, that's when you have a breakthrough."
>
> — MARISSA MAYER, CEO OF YAHOO!

6

"What will my life be like?" How a Great Night can equal a Great Life

"**R**ise and Shine!! The early bird gets the worm!" -my nana, and probably yours too

> "*Morning is an important time of day, because how you spend your morning can often tell you what kind of day you are going to have.*"
>
> — Lemony Snicket

THE MORNING AFTER

You might be wondering why I included this chapter in a book about having a great night out with less alcohol. Now that you're not hungover, what's the point of paying attention to the morning?

There are many reasons. In fact, what you do in the morning and how you start your day can have as much or more impact on your ability to have a great night than what you do in the evening. This is such an important topic that I often start working with my clients on their morning rituals before we talk about their nighttime routine.

Thinking back to my mid and late 20s, I can't remember much of a morning routine. It most likely included the snooze button being pushed at least three times, to-go mugs full of coffee and munching on muffins on the way to work. Those were good days. Bad days were when I slept through my alarm and subsequent meetings because of a crazy night that lasted way too long. Weekends - ahh blessed weekends - were about sleeping in as long as possible, making coffee to drink on the way to brunch, and downing Mimosas or Bloody Marys to take the edge off. Plus, trying to remember the details of the night before was a lot more fun once tipsy (otherwise it was just kind of anxiety-inducing).

I loved mornings, and on yoga retreats or during healthier stints when I could wake up at dawn, I always felt so energized and empowered. However, the reality of my 20's was quite different. I went through long periods where my only rule during my night out was to get home before the birds started chirping. I felt icky if I stayed out until sunrise, which meant a lot of nights ended just before the majority of the population was getting ready to start their next day.

As I began to commit to my "never get wasted again" pact with myself, my relationship to mornings shifted. Waking up without a hangover immediately put me in a good mood, and starting with positivity created a ripple effect throughout the rest of my day. The better my day, the less likely I was to want to get drunk to oblivion at night.

When I began studying wellness, first by self-study and then with the Institute for Integrative Nutrition, I started incorporating more healthy elements into my daily ritual. Soon my morning routine included waking up with the sun, stretching, meditation, journaling, water and lemon juice, and then a green smoothie. It was structured so that I never needed to feel rushed again and became something I looked forward to. I began noticing that my behaviour during the night began to change. "Have another? Hmmmm, no thanks. I know how I want to feel in the morning." My "feel good" baseline shifted, and I created a new normal for myself. Then I began to support others to do the same.

Your morning ritual can include a combination of both physical and mental health benefits. Physical practices could include any combination of the following: water and lemon, green or mate tea, stretching, yoga, dancing or a nature walk. For mental clarity and peace of mind, try yoga, meditation, gratitudes, creative visualization and setting your intentions for the day.

NUTRITION AND WELLNESS TIPS

As I was developing the outline for this book, a friend asked if I was going to include hangover remedies. I struggled with this at first - since the whole point of the book was to serve as a guide to not get wasted... which should mean no hangovers, right?

However, the more I thought about it I realized that the advice I would give to someone who is hungover is essentially the same nutritional advice I would recommend to most people. The only difference is that it is even more important to stick to these guidelines after you've tried one on the night before. Why - because as we all know, waking up hungover is the precursor to craving sugary, carb-laden or fatty foods, which can exacerbate the stress the body is experiencing after too much alcohol. Plus, since this isn't a sobriety guide, and even if it was, there's a good chance that you might hit the bottle a little hard at least one more time in your lifetime.

So, then. Let's imagine that you did over-indulge last night.

You wake up feeling like crap, and the only thing you want to reach for is some sort of fatty/salty/sweet combo that will provide temporary relief. You know it is only temporary relief, but your body has been trained to seek immediate gratification.

This time, I urge you to try something different. Retrain your body and mind to another approach - one that will ultimately get your sparkle back faster, and kiss that head-pounding, bloated, nauseous, zero-energy, listless overall ugh feeling goodbye.

The first step to healing from alcohol over-indulgence is to return the body to an alkaline state. Alcohol, along with sugars, fats, meats and dairy (the stuff we usually crave when we are hungover), makes our bodies overly acidic. Being overly acidic leads us down a slippery slope to more cravings, bad mood, inflammation, and a slew of other health problems.

The fastest way to restore the body's natural pH balance is to overload on alkalizing foods (in addition to limiting the acidic foods listed above). The biggest and easiest category of alkalizing foods is... green foods!! It is preferable to consume your greens first thing in the morning, when your body is thirsting for goodness and ready to absorb every last mineral and vitamin you send its way.

One of the first signals of being overly acidic is low energy. Combined with the cravings and "down" feeling we often get from alcohol overindulgence, it can be hard to think about green foods. However, I promise you, if you follow these next five steps when you wake up on that dreaded day after, your energy will return faster, along with clarity, focus and that radiance you know you have. As I've already mentioned, following these recommendations is also an excellent way to keep yourself in optimum health any day of the week.

1) Start with a glass of water and lemon juice, or water and organic apple cider vinegar, both of which immediately are put to work balancing the pH in your body.

2) Next, drink your greens! First up - a veggie based juice or smoothie (i.e. not sweet) - loaded up with cucumber, celery and leafy greens, all chock full of nutrients, and, you guessed it – super alkalizing. Next up, a green + superfood smoothie. Superfoods (such as spirulina, chia and hemp hearts) are essentially calorie sparse and nutrient dense, meaning you get a lot of nutrition without making your body work hard to get it (and foods that make your body work hard to digest cause, yup – acidity). Now, I realize it's not everyone's favourite thing to be drinking sour (water + lemon) and "earthy" drinks first thing in the morning. It may not satisfy your cravings or fill you up... at least not right away. This process involves training yourself to want different things, and soon the positive benefits from this new way of resolving a hangover will give your body the positive reinforcement she needs. Remind yourself that greens and superfoods are alkalizing and when combined in a delicious smoothie, can give you flavour and fulfillment.

3) Eat the pain away; the healthy way! Throughout the day, eat nutrient dense and satisfying root vegetables, such as sweet potatoes, yams, carrots and beetroot.These vegetables help ground your energy during the potential high and lows you might be experiencing while healing from alcohol overuse. Juicing beetroot (great with carrot and apple added to it) also helps deliver methyl to the liver, which helps detoxify and heal. For breakfast or brunch, try eggs with a sweet potato hash, or poached and served on a bed of greens, with some cubed roasted yams. Add more salads and veggies and healthy fats (nuts and avocado) whenever possible. Keep lots of healthy snacks on hand for when cravings happen.

4) Take supplements. Milk thistle and garlic help the liver. L-glutamine (an amino acid) powder can be added to smoothies or taken in pill form. L-glutamine has been shown to regulate blood sugar levels and help to reduce alcohol and sugar cravings.

5) Rest and Self-love!! Your mindset and mental well-being are just as important as what you are physically putting into your body. Have you noticed that when you are tired or stressed out, you are more likely to reach for comfort foods or succumb to cravings? It is always important to give your body enough rest, and especially important when there is some serious healing going on. So you had a wilder night than you planned? It happens to the best of us. Beating yourself up about it isn't going to make it better. So go gentle, lavish self-love and self-care, and make sure you get enough sleep. We'll go deeper into self-care strategies a little later in this chapter.

The bonus of "living in alkalinity" is that it becomes your body's baseline. Follow these guidelines (not only when you are hungover, but on a daily basis) and instead of craving alcohol, sweets or fatty foods, you'll find yourself craving pH-balanced bliss more and more. If this seems like too drastic of a change all at once, start small and add one new thing to your morning routine each week.

Before she started working with me, my client Shonée's breakfast consisted of diet coke and cigarettes. Even though she knew it was bad for her, she couldn't imagine started her day any other way (and this wasn't just on a hungover day, it was every day). For the first week, she started adding water and lemon and drinking that first thing. Then after 2 weeks, she started with green juices. At first, she thought they were disgusting, now she looks forward to them in the morning. She also added a daily practice of gratitudes and exercising in the morning. Within the span of one month, she had completely changed the way she started her day. Now, instead of dreading mornings, she wakes up energized. Instead of thinking green smoothies are disgusting, she looks forward to them.

MEDITATION

"Half-smile when you first wake up in the morning. Hang a branch, any other sign, or even the word "smile" on the ceiling or wall so that you see it right away when you open your eyes. This sign will serve as your reminder. Use these seconds before you get out of bed to take hold of your breath. Inhale and exhale three breaths gently while maintaining the half smile. Follow your breaths." — Thích Nhất Hạnh, The Miracle of Mindfulness: An Introduction to the Practice of Meditation

Many people will say that they do not have time to meditate. One of the many, many reasons I love Thich Nhat Hanh is that he teaches that it doesn't take much. A few moments of mindfulness, breathing and connecting to your center is always a great way to start your day. Regular meditation is linked to a reduction in stress and worry, and improvement in focus, and as a treatment for relationship problems, addictions and more. Meditation leads to peace of mind, improved well-being, and increased creativity. Who wouldn't want in on that?

One of my clients, Reeta, was a self-professed party queen. As the owner of a successful salon and the lead singer in a band, her life was a whirlwind. She would start the days sleeping in late, rushing out the door and was always forgetting things (including to eat). The chaos continued until she finally came crashing home in the wee hours of the morning, only to repeat it all again the next day.

When she started a morning routine that included between 10-30 minutes of meditation and stretching in the morning, along with tea, water and lemon, a smoothie and prepping her lunch... Her entire day, and night, shifted.

Instead of a whirlwind of chaos, her days felt calmer and more focused. She was more productive and had more time for self-care. By taking time to nourish her body and mind first thing in the morning, she set the tone for the day ahead and found her employees and her partner responding more positively as well.

PRIMING

I like things that come in threes, what can I say? In addition to the practice of the Thrive Threesome described in Chapter 2, I have adapted this practice that I heard Tony Robbins talk about, called priming. He says he starts each day this way, and I've tried it and it works wonders.

Sit in a comfortable position, close your eyes and for the first three minutes, focus on your breath. Inhaling deeply, imagine breathing into the ends of your fingers and tips of your toes, flooding your cells with oxygen. Start by focusing on your gratitudes for three minutes. Then, for the final three-ish minutes, focus on sending love, first to yourself, then let it radiate outwards. Feel the glow for another minute or so. I like to visualize bright gold-white light coming in through the top of my head, and as I exhale, the light radiates outward and touches everything and everyone to whom I am sending light. Try it! It's a beautiful way to start the day. As Tony Robbins says, "If you don't have 10 minutes, you don't have a life... there's no excuse."

GRATITUDES

We already covered the importance of gratitudes in Chapter 2, but in my view the practice of gratitude is so valuable that it is worth repeating here. I'm sure you've heard the idiom about "getting up on the wrong side of the bed," which, of course, means starting the day irritable, unhappy, uncomfortable and dare I say, bitchy?

Even if you are hungover, short of sleep because there was a party next door that you valiantly tried to sleep through, there were sirens all night, or you were binge-watching Netflix until four in the morning - temporarily forgetting that you had an early meeting with your boss at work... Whatever the reason - gratitudes can help shift from the wrong foot to the right foot.

You can practice gratitudes while still laying in bed... wiggle your toes and stretch your limbs and feel gratitude for your body. Notice the sun shining through the window. Think about the fact you survived the night and woke up alive. Appreciate that special someone in your life or someone who did something nice for you. Or think about the food you have in your fridge, or even the fact that you have an iPad and working internet to be able to watch Netflix. There are infinite reasons to be grateful, and starting the day with appreciation, counting your blessings and saying thanks is like getting on the superhighway to happiness.

> *"If the only prayer you said in your whole life was, "thank you," that would suffice."*
>
> — MEISTER ECKHART

JOURNALING/MORNING PAGES

After pouring yourself a cup of tea, spending a few minutes journaling can also really help center and focus your day. This is where you can set your intentions for the day, or do your Thrive Threesome as described in Chapter 2. Again, it doesn't need to take long - a few minutes to jot down your thoughts, intentions, gratitudes and desires can be enough.

Julia Cameron, the creator of the Artist's Way, recommended what she calls The Morning Pages, which is a free write stream of consciousness. Morning Pages provoke, clarify, comfort, prioritize and synchronize the day at hand. Do not over-think Morning Pages. As Julie writes, just put "three pages of anything on the page...and then do three more pages tomorrow."

ACTION STEPS

1. Spend a few moments answering the following in your journal: What is one thing you can do differently, starting tomorrow? What would you like to include in your morning routine?

2. Next, write out your morning routine and put it next to your bed! Set your alarm for 15 minutes earlier, and set your intention to get up early. When I know I have limited time the following morning, I often prep my green smoothie the night before. Having a meditation pillow or designated area for meditation can also help inspire.

3. Finally, don't forget that you don't need anything to start your day with gratitude or a few moments of mindfulness, you can do this from your bed. You simply need to decide to start doing it. Set a reminder to alert at the same time as your alarm, so that you don't "forget" and hit snooze again instead of using those precious first moments to set the tone for your day.

"Life is too short," she panicked, *"I want more."* He nodded slowly, *"Wake up earlier."*

—Dr. SunWolf

7

"Do I have to do this alone?"

Communication and Relationships

*It takes a great deal of bravery to stand up to our enemies,
but just as much to stand up to our friends.*

— J. K. ROWLING

One of the topics that arises most often is how to address this topic with the people around you. This chapter covers what to say to the randoms at the bar, whose opinion really shouldn't matter yet somehow we always end up feeling we have to explain ourselves. Perhaps even more importantly, we'll discuss how to talk to friends, family, and loved ones.

PART 1 - FOR THE RANDOMS AND ACQUAINTANCES

I get asked a lot about one-liners. No, not those one-liners. I've never been one of those master pick-up artists who knows exactly what to say to hook that mysterious stranger from across the bar. I'm talking about the one-liners that you can use to detract invasive and at times belligerent questions about why you aren't drinking.

The first time I decided to stop drinking and then decided to venture back into my social scene sans-alcohol, it was intimidating. I stumbled over my words. I felt like I needed to justify my actions. I over-explained myself at times. I opened the door for a dialogue I didn't necessarily feel like having in the middle of a noisy bar or party.

What I also found was that the people who were drinking would very quickly make the issue about themselves. They'd take it personally that I didn't want to drink with/like them. Seeing someone choose differently is sometimes like having a mirror held up, and I've found that most people aren't ready to look at what they see.

Over the years, though, I've learned several strategies that have worked for me in situations like this (and these are the ones that I share with my clients, as well).

But before we dive into the one-liners, it is important to remind yourself that it is no one's business if you're drinking alcohol or not. More importantly, it's no one's business why you aren't drinking alcohol. Period. You do not owe anyone an explanation, so release yourself from feeling like you do, right now.

The thing is, if someone offers you a drink or asks why you aren't drinking, and your response is, "I don't drink," the follow-up question will almost always be, "Why?" That's why it is good to have a few of these one-liners ready for delivery.

Second, drunk people or people who may have an issue/problem with alcohol will often try to make whatever you are saying about them - so choose your words carefully. Make it about you, not them. Even if they start personalizing whatever you're saying, you can go so far as to say, "This really isn't about you, enjoy your drink! There's no judgment over here."

Before we dive in, I must say that I'm not a huge fan of lying. There's a lot of advice out there on how to avoid prying questions about your non-drinking, and many advocate lying. Sure, there's a time and a place, like maybe when talking to an intrusively creepy stranger ("I'm pregnant!" often works like a charm in this scenario). There's also a lot of excuses you can use, such as "I'm driving!" or "I have an important meeting tomorrow" or "I'm allergic" or "I'm on antibiotics" ... but I find these set you up for some internalized shame. By not being at least somewhat honest, you are telling yourself there is something about which to be ashamed. You should never feel ashamed about your decision not to drink alcohol.

I'm an advocate of being as aligned as possible with your truth.

Owning and speaking the truth about your experience is a signal to the greater forces (call it God, the Universe, whatever works for you) that you are taking yourself seriously.

So whatever your reasons are for not drinking or wanting to drink less, give yourself some credit and an energetic boost that affirms the path you are on. If you need a refresher, check Chapter 2 again and redo the activity.

Okay, so what are some of my favourite one-liners? Drumroll please - here they are (in order of most vague to more specific):

I'm just taking a break for a while.
Why it works: You are clearly making this statement about yourself. You aren't making absolute statements; you aren't saying alcohol is bad (which often triggers people), and you aren't saying this is forever. You don't need to go into details, but if pressed for more, you can respond with the following one-liner.

1) It started affecting me differently, so I decided to cut it out for a while.

    Why it works: Again, you are making a statement with which no one can argue. You aren't saying that alcohol is good or bad, only that you started feeling it differently and are making different choices.

2) For health reasons.

    Why it works: It's vague, and again, difficult for someone to challenge your personal quest for better health. They may retort that "Wine is good for you," or "There's nothing wrong with one drink" at which point you could follow up with the next one-liner.

3) I'm doing a cleanse. (or insert another health-related initiative)

    Why it works: With so many different kinds of cleanses and "detox" programs out there - most people are familiar with the concept of cutting out certain foods or substances for a while. And it's the truth! If you are pressed with further questions or feel like elaborating, you can talk about all of the health-related reasons you are giving your body a break from alcohol.

4) I'm doing my own personal social experiment, I want to learn what it feels like to be in XX situation without alcohol.

    Why it works: This sometimes confuses drunk people, because they start thinking about what it might be like looking in from the more sober side of things. This is where you make your escape. Okay, but seriously, I've had good results with this one - again, it's a personal statement grounded in curiosity and investigation.

5) I'm in the process of getting to know myself better, so I decided to cut out alcohol for a while.

    Why it works: Similarly to number 5, this is a "pause and think about it" kind of answer.

6) If the asker challenges you with something along the lines of, "And you really think you need to stop drinking to do that?" Your answer can be a simple, "Yes, I'll let you know what I find out."

Of course, there are a million other ways to turn down a drink. Quite often a simple, "I'm good for now, thanks!" delivered with a smile will suffice, but being able to share the whole truth, if you feel comfortable, is always fantastic.

The more we can support each other to open up about the reasons why we're deciding to drink less alcohol (or none at all!), the more we are creating awareness that there are alternatives to alcohol-fuelled fun.

PART 2 - FOR THE LOVED ONES

You can use all of the one-liners above when it comes to someone you are dating, your friends or family. I have many clients who haven't felt like getting into the nitty gritty just yet. They opt for slightly vague explanations, like doing a cleanse or "for health reasons" rather than offering a longer more in-depth explanation.

It is important to remember that this is your journey. You don't owe anyone else an explanation. Sometimes it is easier to understand what these changes mean to you first before trying to explain to those around you.

However, it can also be incredibly helpful to confide in a few supportive people. As talked about in Chapter 3, having others who can help us stay accountable to ourselves is critical to our Drink Less Success.

One of the most common challenges my clients face in this area is that their friends and family are resistant to them changing. Quite often, it is because those people are still drinking and do not consider it problematic in their lives, or they aren't ready to admit that it is.

It is incredibly important to remember that you are the only one that gets to define your relationship to alcohol and what it means to you. You may not have a "problem" in the eyes of those around you, or according to society's standards or definitions of problematic drinking or alcoholism, but that doesn't matter. It is about you, your body, your health and well-being.

Your friends, family or significant other may be resistant to you making changes because it may force them to look at their drinking that they may not be ready to do. There may be cultural or familial expectations around drinking, especially during events, celebrations, and special occasions. Your parents might wonder if they are at fault, and personalize your decision to cut back on your drinking, or might take it as an affront to their own preferred behaviour.

This can be tricky territory to navigate, and it is always really important to come back to your internal compass to help you navigate what feels right to share with those closest to you. Finding that one person with whom you can confide can be helpful. Remember to focus on your own experience and reasons for doing this. Use "I statements" and avoid making judgements about others that may cause them to feel defensive.

Some people might feel like by asking them to be supportive, you might be asking them to change as well. Be as clear as you can with your request for support - show them how they can best support you.

Examples might include:

"I'm trying to cut back on my drinking so that I don't keep blacking out. I would appreciate your support this Friday night to help me stick to my three drink limit, and to remind me to drink water in between."

"Babe, as much as I love sharing a bottle of wine with you before we go to the bar, I'd love to find an alternative to this. I find that when I drink before going out, I'm more likely to keep drinking more than I want to through the night, and it's really hard to stick to my fitness goals when I feel hungover the next day."

"Hey sis, I'd love your support for our family BBQ this Sunday. I'm doing a partial cleanse right now and trying to keep my drinking to a minimum for a while. You know how we can all get kind of carried away. I don't want this to be a big deal with the rest of the family, but I could really use your help not to hit the mojitos too hard. I'm going to be making non-alcoholic ones until after dinner, because if I get day-drunk I'll mess up my intentions."

As the date of her bachelorette party approached, one of my clients became quite nervous as to how she was going to handle the pressure to drink. "My girlfriends are quite wild, and I don't think they will go easy on me." While she wanted to have a great time and didn't want to make it a big deal, she also didn't want to suffer for days after. She had been practicing her Drink Less intentions for awhile, and her tolerance was lower. As a solution, she enlisted her sister and best friend as her Sip Sisters for the evening, asking them to pour her non-alcoholic drinks and try to hold off on rounds of shots.

Taking the steps to change can be scary, especially when it seems like you might alienate the people that matter most in your life. It is true that I have seen relationships end when one person decides to drink less, and their significant other isn't prepared to change. I have also seen the opposite - relationships that thrive when one person commits to their health, and the other person eventually decides to embrace that change as well.

Just as reading the information in this book isn't going to help you change unless you want to, your readiness to change will not make another person ready to change unless he or she is ready. The best you can do is keep taking the steps that feel best for you and your health.

FOMO

"In my drinking days I had to be at every party, every get-together, every "Dollar Shots Night" at the bar and any other occasion that involved social drinking," writes Kelly Fitzgerald, the woman behind the blog The Sober Señorita. "The irrational fear I experienced was that if I didn't show up at one of these events I would miss out on something important. As they say, 'the struggle is real.' This fear motivated my drinking and going-out habits for many years."

It's common when we start making these changes to get a vicious case of "Fear of Missing Out" every now and again. What will I miss if I go home early? What crazy adventure will I be left out of if I'm not as drunk as my friends? What if I miss the best dancing of my life? What if the person of my dreams is waiting for me at the after-hours?

Whenever you feel FOMO rear its nasty head, take a few deep breaths. Rather than focusing on everything you think you might be missing out on, remind yourself of all the positive outcomes that you are inviting into your life.

ACTION STEPS:

1. Take a few moments to write down all of the reasons you decided to change your drinking habits.
2. Decide which one-liner will work best for you, or adapt one so that it feels right for your unique situation.
3. Consider who is close to you that you might be able to talk to about the change that you want to make and ask for support. This could be your Sip Sister, best friend, drinking buddy, significant other.

4. Arrange a time to chat with that person and write down a few points you'd like to share with them in advance so that you feel well prepared. You may also want to send them an email, clearly outlining how they can best support you.

"A friend is someone who knows all about you and still loves you."

— ELBERT HUBBARD

8

"The thought of sober sex freaks me out" Alcohol and Intimacy: Once you change you'll never go back!

Let's talk about sex, baby

— SALT N PEPA

How could I write a guide to having a great time without getting wasted without addressing the topic of dating and sex? This is such a huge and complex subject that it deserves its own book, but I will try to do it justice in the space we have here.

In my rather informal polling of friends and clients, the majority have used alcohol more often than not in dating and the initial stages of their intimate relationships. While speaking with a colleague and fellow health coach recently, she mused "Come to think of it, I think alcohol was involved in all my relationships until my current one."

Alcohol is used as an icebreaker, a way to allow ourselves access to our desires, the social lubricants that shuts up the voices in our head and helps us confidently embody something more primal. If you have ever used alcohol to help with your hook-ups, you are certainly not alone.

As Rebecca Reid challenges in a recent Daily Telegraph article about sober sex, "if you're ever in the mood to really scare yourself then I'd suggest sitting down and trying to work out how many times you've had sex whilst you were sober. Stone cold sober."

It's a tough one, isn't it? Without assigning a judgment as to whether it is a "good" or "bad" thing - it is an interesting exercise to consider the role that alcohol has played in your sex life. Looking back at the combination of my sexual and drinking history, my current partner is the first person with whom our first sex was "stone cold sober." I was in my early thirties by then. I know many other women in their late thirties and 40s who still rely on alcohol to allow them to feel comfortable with their sexual partners.

The subject of the role alcohol and other substances play in our sex lives has always really interested me, so much so that as one of my final papers in my Psychology major in college, I conducted a qualitative study of how young women used alcohol to explore their sexuality. I found, not surprisingly, that using alcohol had both positive and negative outcomes for the women I interviewed.

Consider the following two scenarios.

Larissa is getting ready for a date. To calm her nerves and give herself an extra boost of confidence, she pours herself a vodka soda while getting ready. The pour is probably a little heavy handed - so she's already feeling a bit of a buzz when her date picks her up. At the restaurant, they have another cocktail while waiting to be seated, then share a bottle of wine with dinner. They decide to skip dessert and at the suggestion of her date, head to a lounge or bar. Though by this point Larissa is feeling well on her way to getting drunk, she says yes when her date asks if she'd like another drink.

Sana is at the bar with a group of her girlfriends. The night is alright, but not too exciting. As she glances around the dimly lit room at the couples intermingling and dancing, she feels a deep sense of yearning. She scans the room, looking for someone who peaks her desire. She's already downed a few doubles and after a round of shots with her friends, she feels the confidence to return the gaze of a guy who has been checking her out from across the room. She smiles, he approaches, they dance, he offers her a drink. Pretty soon, they are in the taxi, tumbling into kissing, then up the stairs to her apartment. While he excuses himself to go to the bathroom, Sana rushes to the kitchen to take a long deep swig from the bottle of vodka she keeps in the freezer. The burn as the straight alcohol rushes down her throat brings immediate relief. She pops a breath mint into her mouth. She's ready.

Do you see yourself in either of these scenarios or a combination of the two? What about your friends? According to a study by the American Psychological Association, women are significantly more likely to have sex with a partner they have just met in an encounter involving alcohol than in an encounter not involving alcohol. I guess you already knew that fact, didn't you?

We use alcohol to lower inhibitions and increase confidence, to experience openness to try new things, to give ourselves permission to express our desires, to achieve a feeling of closeness, and to get the nagging puritan voices in our heads to shut up. There are probably many other "good reasons" to use alcohol in our dating and sex lives, and it is entirely understandable why so many women do it.

The unfortunate flip side is that a little too much of a good thing can quickly lead us down a darker path of increased sexual risk, including sexual health risk, unplanned pregnancy, unwanted attention and sexual violence.

Something we don't actually hear about often is that while alcohol might lower inhibitions and help get you in the mood, too much alcohol actually restricts blood flow to your vagina, causes dehydration and actually makes it more difficult to self-lubricate. Because alcohol is a central nervous system depressant and can dull and impair nerve sensation in other parts of your body, so too will it dull the nerves and sensations most needed to help you orgasm.

In a sense, by drinking more than 1 or 2 drinks before hooking up, you might be creating a self-defeating situation, whereby your body doesn't respond the way your intoxicated mind might want.

In the examples above, Larissa and Sana's names could have been exchanged for my own and it would have summed up most of my 20s and early 30s. Eventually, the time came when I started to want more. More connection, more presence, more sensation and of course, a clear memory of everything that had transpired. I wanted to feel sure of myself, to know that what I was doing with another person actually meant something, that it was something I actually wanted and wanted enough to be able to do it sober.

This was new territory for me. In a sense, I felt like I was traveling back in time, trying out dating and sexuality again for the first time (even from a young age, alcohol had been involved for me). While nerve-wracking, my new way of being was also exhilarating.

The following list is a combination of strategies that I have used and that my clients have used when they've decided to try something different and add the sobriety spice to their dating and sex life.

STRATEGIES

Getting ready

Create new rituals for getting yourself ready, psyched, confident and feeling your best before heading out. Put on your best anthems, say your mantras or affirmations, treat yourself to a sensual bubble bath, get yourself a mini-aromatherapy massage, make a delicious elixir to sip. In short, give yourself the goddess treatment. Review Chapter 4 if you need more inspiration for getting ready for your date.

Stop trying to find a date at the bar

Instead of relying on the bar to meet people - get more creative! Use this challenge as your opportunity to try new and exciting activities where you'll have a chance of meeting a special someone that's more in line with your health goals. Been wanting to try a new sport or hobby for a while? Now's the time.

Switch up the venue

When you do get asked on a date, suggest something other than an evening date at a restaurant or bar. It helps to make a list of cool date ideas ahead of time so that you are ready with an alternative suggestion.

"There's this new brunch spot I've wanted to try, why don't we meet there?"

"You know that I haven't been to the planetarium in since I was a kid? Have you? Would you like to meet me there?"

"It's supposed to be sunny this weekend, and I've been stuck in the office all weekend. Why don't we meet at the park?"

Brush up on your one-liners

If you do end up on a date at a restaurant, the first time the waiter arrives and asks if you'd like to see the wine list can be uncomfortable. Knowing what alternative drink you'd like to order and asking for it confidently rather than stammering "I'll just have water please" will help ease any awkwardness. If I know the restaurant I'm going to in advance, I'll often check out their menu online. "I've wanted to try that aloe-basil beverage you have, that sounds interesting." Your date may not even notice that you haven't ordered alcohol.

If you do get asked why you aren't drinking, it helps to know in advance how you want to answer the question. Again, preparation is everything. Review the one-liners in Chapter 7 for more tips.

Flirting/texting and sexting

Instead of waiting for someone to initiate flirting with you, taking the lead can bring a rush similar to the effects of alcohol. If you'd like, practice first on the cashier at the grocery store, and build up towards what you'd like to say to your object of desire. Becoming a temptress texter can also help build the sexual desire and tension. Sometimes it feels safer to text your desires rather than to speak them, so this is a great transition to practice communicating your desires sober.

Mood lighting

You know when you're drunk, and the edges blur, and everything is slightly unfocused. You stop caring - or don't even notice - whether the lights are on or off? You can create this sensation with candles, darker lighting, dimmer switches and bulbs with a warmer, reddish glow. Scented candles or essential oil infusions are also a great way to rev up the sensory experience and set the tone.

Mood music

The nice thing about being drunk is that the voice in your head shuts up and all of a sudden you don't care if there's anyone within earshot of your sexing. Picking the right music can help you emulate that feeling. Make a sexy playlist in advance full of songs that remind you of wild, raunchy times.

Keep focusing on the best possible outcome

It can be nerve-wracking the first time to try to go on a date or have sex sober. Even if you are having sex with a long time lover or partner, it is easy to fall into self-doubt or anxiety around how it will be. Try to focus on the best possible outcome, rather than all the ways it could go wrong. The positive visualization tips in Chapter 2 can help with this.

Communication is key

Vulnerability might be scary, but it's also sexy. When I finally felt comfortable sharing with my intimate partner the fact that having sex sober made me nervous, it allowed him to treat me, and our sex, differently. He became even more invested in making sure it was the best possible experience for me. Feeling this trust build opened up my confidence to be able to express my sexual desires, to tell him what felt good and what didn't, to slow things down or speed things up. I began to be able to truly tap into what felt right for that moment.

Treat it like it's your first time

If you've been seeing someone for awhile, but it is the first time you are having sex sober, consider what it might be like if you treat it like it's the first time - ever. This can be incredibly hot, and incredibly healing, especially for those of us whose firsts were less than stellar. Imagine getting a re-do, a new introduction to your sex life, taking all of the experience and self-knowledge you've amassed along the way.

My first time having sex was so far from my fantasy that it still feels tragic. When I think about what my revised fairy-tale version would be, it involves planning with nervous anticipation, lots of romancing before, candles, silky sheets, sensual massage and hours of seduction and exploration. How beautiful would it be to create that safe space with your lover, to experience your first sober sex? There is no need to downplay the significance - it is a big deal and can be treated as such.

Switch it up/try something new/somewhere new

Once you are feeling more confident with your sober sexing, and if you start missing the wild romps of your drunken days, consider switching things up and trying something new. New positions, new locations - like somewhere that feels risque or taboo.

Don't keep alcohol in the house

If you are tempted to chug booze before getting hot and heavy in the bedroom, consider emptying your fridge and cupboards of any temptation. It is far easier to flush your intentions down the drain if you've had a glass or two of wine during dinner and feel your nerves kick in once you are back home.

Keep a few mantras ready in the bathroom and give yourself a few moments to remind yourself how beautiful, confident and sexy you are. Again, focus on everything that can go right, and the best possible outcome, and take a few deep breaths to relax.

Next!!

If your date or lover cannot respect the fact that you've decided to make some changes around your alcohol use, the chances are they aren't your forever-person. If they try to belittle or question your decision or pressure you to drink more than you want to, it might be time to say "see-ya".

At the risk of sounding glib, I know this can be easier said than done. However, now more than ever, it is important to surround yourself with people who support your decisions and your desire to be your healthiest self. The person you are with should be willing to be patient and get to know the new you (and how much fun, clear minded and confident you will be). If they aren't, then it might be time to let go. Move on to a love that is truly supportive of the path you are on.

ACTIVITY:

1. Journal your experiences around alcohol and intimacy. What have been the positive experiences that you would like to recreate? What have been the negative experiences that you are ready to let go of? Why do you want to keep alcohol out of your intimate relationships?
2. Set your intentions, revisit Chapter 1.
3. Revisit the visualization in Chapter 1, focusing on your date or intimacy

"All intimacy is rare — that's what makes it precious. And it involves the revelation of one's self and the loving gaze upon another's true self (no makeup, no fancy car, no defensive charm, no seduction) — that's what makes it so damn hard. Intimacy requires honesty and kindness in almost equal measure (a little more kindness, I think), trust and trustworthiness, forgiveness and the capacity to be forgiven . . . It's more than worth it — just don't let them tell you it's bliss."

— AMY BLOOM

9

What about binges and blackouts?
Your body and your brain

"I cannot teach anybody anything. I can only make them think."

— SOCRATES

THE BEHAVIOUR

There are many books and websites dedicated to the effects of alcohol on your body that provide more detail than the scope of this guide. I'm sure you don't need me to tell you that the more you drink, the greater your risk of cancers, strokes, heart disease, infertility, liver disease, pancreatitis, and a compromised immune system. You probably would not have picked up this book if you didn't already have a sense that the amount you are drinking might be causing you some harm.

I was in denial about the potential damage I was causing myself for some years. I also directed my assumptions of who would be negatively affected by alcohol to people who drank way more than myself. Though I went through periods of daily drinking, it wasn't my "thing." I didn't have a physical dependence, therefore, how much harm could I really be doing?

As it turns out, even a couple of nights or weekends of hard partying can seriously stress your system.

The information in this chapter relates to people like us - it is about the effects of alcohol on those who like to have a great time, and sometimes get carried away. When I was finally ready to change my ways, learning how alcohol was affecting my body helped me commit to kicking the "get wasted out of my senses" habit for good.

Does the following scenario sound familiar?

For the most part, you take it easy with alcohol. A drink or two with dinner, possibly a nightcap after a long day, but nothing excessive - because you don't want drinking to interfere with your busy work lives or productivity, right? That is, until the opportunity arises. You time it perfectly - usually on a weekend - no immediate work responsibilities the next day. You've been saving up for this all week- and when you let go, you go hard.

Work hard, play hard - right? After all, you deserve it.

The next day, you'll drink a green juice, hit the gym, sweat it out and be back to normal. Maybe.

Maybe not. Research on the neurocognitive effects of alcohol (outlined later in this chapter) shows how bingeing is bad for your brain, and it might not be for the reasons you think.

Yes, there are the immediate consequences that we're all aware of: the pounding head, the fogginess, the underlying nausea. Those are symptoms that can be treated fairly quickly, leading us to feel like we're back to "normal" quicker than we actually are.

But before we go there, let's talk about what exactly constitutes binge drinking.

The National Institute of Alcohol Abuse and Alcoholism (NIAAA) defines binge drinking as a pattern of drinking that brings a person's blood alcohol concentration (BAC) to 0.08 grams percent or above. This typically happens when men co-nsume 5 or more drinks, and when women consume 4 or more drinks, in about 2 hours. (A drink would be a small glass of wine or beer, or a cocktail with 1 oz of alcohol.)

As you can see, it is quite easy to ingest that amount of alcohol, or more, in a big night out. What's more is that, if you are anything like me, it didn't stop at one night. There would be brunch the next day, then maybe a happy hour, drinks with dinner, and another night out, followed by another brunch on Sunday. In short, a lot of alcohol over a short span of time.

I used to think that by Monday I could be back to normal again, but research shows I was mistaken. Now, I'm not usually one for scare tactics - but the more I started researching this info, the more I felt like I needed to share.

BINGEING AND YOUR BRAIN

"I would not put a thief in my mouth to steal my brains."

— WILLIAM SHAKESPEARE, OTHELLO

Dr Jonathan Chick, of the Alcohol Problems Service at the Royal Edinburgh Hospital and the chief editor of "Alcohol and Alcoholism", says his research shows that "humans who have a few heavy drinking sessions in a row may sometimes undergo subtle brain changes which make it both harder to learn from mistakes and harder to learn new ways of tackling problems because their brain function has been subtly impaired."

Another interesting study, conducted by two identical twin brothers, Chris and Alexander van Tullekens, who also happen to be doctors, was the focus of a recent BBC Horizon special.

Alexander drank three units of alcohol daily, whereas Chris consumed the weekly amount of alcohol in a span of 24 hours, four times (weekends) in a month. The aim was to see how the same quantity of alcohol affected the body, given the difference in the way it was consumed.

Chris reports feeling his experiment would be easier. He thought he would deal with a day or two of hangover, and then feel great the rest of the week. The results, however, showed otherwise. "My levels of cytokines and interleukins, those key markers of inflammation, were raised. I'd expected them to be sky high after the first binge - but six days later, just before I was about to start the second binge, they hadn't gone down at all, and at the end of four weeks they'd soared."

Well, there goes the idea that a week off in between a big binge is enough to clear the system. He continues, "I felt good but my body was still damaged from the binge. Inflammation is linked to a vast array of diseases from cancer and severe infection to heart disease and dementia. This was not a good result."

In a National Institute for Alcohol and Addictions publication on alcohol and Alzheimer disease, Dr Suzanne Tyas writes that while there is still more research needed on whether alcohol use can be a predictor for Alzheimer's, it is proved that some of the detrimental effects of heavy alcohol use on brain function are similar to those observed in Alzheimer's disease. Heavy drinking accelerates shrinkage, or atrophy of the brain, which causes neurodegenerative changes... in other words, brain damage. Ugh.

Dr Fulton T. Crews, professor in the Department of Pharmacology and Psychiatry at the University of North Carolina at Chapel Hill, says that "there are growing list of studies that suggest that even short-term binge drinking can have long-term effects."

> "When your body hits an inflammatory overload, your defense system gets so overwhelmed and confused that it literally doesn't know the difference between the invader and you. As a result, your well-meaning immune system turns on itself, destroying healthy cells, tissue, and everything else in its wake. It's like when Al Pacino played Tony Montana in Scarface. He mows down everything in sight, yelling, "Say hello to my little friend!" In a word: shit."

— KRIS CARR, CRAZY SEXY KITCHEN

Before you spiral into doom and gloom, "well if I'm already brain damaged then what's the point I may as well continue boozing and at least have fun while I'm dumbing myself down" - let me stop you right there. That kind of fatalism will get you nothing more than a foggier brain with less functional brain cells, a body rife with inflammation, and an overburdened liver.

There is hope! The good news is that, unlike Alzheimer's and terminal cancer, you can turn this around. Studies show that the atrophy of brain cells decreases after abstinence from alcohol (but it can take up to a year!), and what we know from many cancer survivors is that adopting an "anti-inflammatory lifestyle" can reduce or halt the progression of inflammation-induced ailments. Does it mean you have to give up alcohol forever? No. Does it mean making some lifestyle changes? Yes, of course. Trust me, your brain and body will thank you for it.

Here are some recommended tips for cutting back in the long term, and eventually changing your drink-to-excess tendencies.

TAKING A BREAK

Try a period of abstinence. My friend Jina Schaefer, a health coach who leads regular 40 day alcohol free challenges on Facebook, recommends giving yourself a little over a month to press the reset, and really look at your relationship to alcohol. Remember, it doesn't have to be forever. However, this step is only helpful if followed up by the next steps. Taking a period of time off of alcohol should not be treated as permission to jump right back into the same heavy drinking as before, and doing so can actually lead to your break causing more harm than good.

STICK TO THE RECOMMENDED DAILY AMOUNT

As someone who is a bit "authority-averse" at times (ok, a lot), this is a tough one for me. "What do 'they' know?," I used to think to myself. "My tolerance is great!" Well, just because I could hold my alcohol didn't mean it wasn't harming my body and brain. The government guidelines are there for a reason. The reason isn't a Big Brotherish buzzkill, it's because drinking more than the recommended guidelines has been shown to have serious health risks (such as risk of cancer, heart disease, etc.). So ladies, that means no more than 3 standard sized drinks a night, according to the Canadian guidelines for low-risk drinking.

Remember Chapter 5, where we discussed knowing when "enough is enough?" That concept applies here as well. It's important for you to learn what your internal tipping point is. If you know that by the time you are on your 3rd drink that you've crossed the point of no return, it might be time to set your nightly limit to two drinks to avoid slipping into a habitual binge.

PACE YOURSELF (BYE BYE BINGEING)

As discussed in chapter 5 - Alternate one alcoholic drink with two non-alcoholic drinks. Then experiment with different drinking behaviours. If you feel like you want to treat yourself to one or two drinks during the week so that you aren't saving up for the big blowout on the weekend, try that. As Dr Michael Wilks says "Saving up your weekly units so you can drink them all on a Friday night is not the way to interpret the government's advice."

LIVE AN ANTI-INFLAMMATION LIFESTYLE

This is a biggie and involves more than just cutting back on alcohol. The "work hard play hard" lifestyle often puts stress on our system in a myriad of ways, and we now know that stress is inflammatory as well. Strive to achieve a bit more balance, get 30 minutes more sleep a night, enjoy restful, relaxing and regenerative activities like yoga, meditation, swimming, walking in nature, and eating a plant-based and nutrient dense diet. If you do have a big night out, reconsider reaching for a burger the next day and try a green juice, root veggies or salad instead (all anti-inflammatory). Most importantly - don't beat yourself up!! If anything, pamper yourself more.

TAKE 5 (OR 10)

Find ways to take mini-breaks or as Katie Corcoran, founder of Thrive and Hustle calls them, "hustle breaks." Break the binge behaviour by allowing yourself pleasure play dates throughout your days and weeks so that you don't feel the need to go "all out" on the weekend. Surround yourself with beauty, have fresh flowers at your desk and remind yourself to smell them, keep floral aromatherapy scents on hand to get you out of your head and into the moment, take dance or spin classes, anything that gives you the opportunity to get out of your head and into your body.

For those of us women who push ourselves hard - too hard sometimes, - alcohol becomes the permission slip; the hall pass that allows us to check out for a while. For many years drinking to excess to escape my overwhelmed brain then spending my only day off curled up in fetal position was the only way I knew how to give myself permission to "check out".

Geneen Roth, who writes on the topic of bingeing in relationship to food, puts it brilliantly in an excerpt from "Binge Trace: Interrupted:"

"We need to give ourselves permission to check out from the frantic, overwhelming pace of our lives. If you watch small children, you'll see that they race around madly and then collapse. They put out huge amounts of energy, and then they need to rest. We're like that, too, but we've forgotten about the downtime part. We think we can be on the run endlessly and be fine.

Wrong.

The rhythm of exertion needs to be followed by rest. There is a time to run around and a time to plunge into oblivion. If we don't build the latter into our lives, we suffer. Either we become utterly exhausted or we sneak a plunge on the sly, sometimes while sitting in a car at a gas station. We grab time for ourselves by bingeing, and because we don't feel we're allowed the luxury of downtime, we end up hurting ourselves."

I had to teach myself to be okay with down time, to treat myself to hustle breaks, to find ways to get out of my head that didn't involve being obliterated by alcohol or collapsing in exhaustion. I had to learn that I am a worthy human being - even in my downtime. In fact, my downtime is vital to my ability to recharge. My body and brain are better for it. I can guarantee that yours will be too.

OUR BIOLOGY AND BLACKOUTS

"I walk through the front door of my hotel, alone. It's that time of night when every floor has a banana peel and, if I'm not careful, I might find my face against the ground, my hands braced beside me. I exchange a few pleasantries with the concierge, a bit of theatre to prove I'm not too drunk. The last thing I hear is my heels, steady as a metronome, echoing through the lobby. And then there is nothing.

This happens to me sometimes. A curtain falling in the middle of the act, leaving minutes and sometimes hours in the dark. But anyone watching me wouldn't notice. They'd simply see a woman on her way to somewhere else, with no idea her memory just snapped in half."

Sarah Hepola, author of Blackout: Remembering The Things I Drank To Forget

When I first read this passage, it gave me the chills.

I have had more blackouts that I can count. For me, blackouts were the ugly, scary result of "too much fun." The irony is that too much fun led to shame, regret, and grief - an aching sadness over significant periods of time "lost" with no means of recollection.

Many of my clients come to me with similar experiences. Blackouts are listed as one of the worst negative consequences of their drinking. For many women, the goal is learning how to manage their alcohol so that they can go out, drink, have a great time and remember every second of it.

Blackouts seem to start at a blood alcohol content of around .20, and women often reach that level quicker than men, which means that we are more prone to blackouts. Why does this happen?

In her article "Anatomy of a Blackout" Julie Beck writes that women have less alcohol dehydrogenase in our guts—an enzyme that helps break down alcohol. The effect: a woman will likely absorb about 30% more alcohol into her bloodstream than a man of the same weight who has consumed an equal amount. We also have less free-floating water in our bodies than men do, and since alcohol disperses in body water, we maintain a higher concentration for longer. Simply put, if you are going shot for shot with a dude at the bar, you are going to get way more wasted, and be much more likely to blackout.

The Canadian Centre for Substance Abuse describes low-risk drinking as no more than three drinks a night for women, and four drinks a night for men. I used to think this was "crazy low" - something concocted by the fun police rather than put in place to provide sound health recommendations. The more I researched, I also realized the guidelines are not meant to oppress women and take away our freedom to drink as much as men. As Drinkaware. uk writes, "It's not sexism, it's biology."

While it's hard to know the exact number of women who suffer blackouts because so many go unreported, recent studies of college students show that 1 in 4 students who drink alcohol will experience a blackout.

With so many of us dealing secretly with the shame of a blackout, we often lack solutions when the only one presented is a loud "if you have problems then don't drink."

All of the strategies outlined in this book will help you avoid blackouts. Anytime you need a refresher, just re-read Chapters 4 and 5 to remember the strategies that will help you wake up with your memories of the night before intact.

It is also important to do the inner work necessary to avoid repeating the same cycles. If you have experienced a blackout in the past and have lingering feelings of shame, regret, embarrassment or sadness, give yourself some extra love and forgiveness. Reach out, share your story with a trusted friend, your partner, coach, therapist or Sip Sister.

If you are a friend on the receiving end of hearing of someone else's blackout, make sure to offer them safety, non-judgment and support instead of laughing it off or minimizing it.

We know that stuffing these feelings will keep setting ourselves up for the kind of artificial release that comes with alcohol, then drinking too much again to escape our brains or the pain, and the cycle continues.

ACTIONS STEPS:

1. Have you experienced any of these harmful side effects of drinking? Take a moment and write down what they were like. Be gentle with yourself, as bringing up these memories and experiences can be difficult.
2. Now, forgive yourself. Release any guilt, shame embarrassment or other negative feelings you may be holding on to. They no longer serve you.
3. Write down three things that you know now that you didn't know then, and three ways you will do things differently. Locate the power within you to create change and a different outcome the next time around.

10

What if work hard/play hard is my "mo"? - Developing a Drink Less Be More Life Philosophy

As you read in the title of this guide, the goal is to create a life worth remembering. By setting your intentions for a great night, you start living your best life, day by day. I've learned that it is an excellent way to live - you truly get the best of both worlds. All the fun, remembering every detail, and a healthier mind, body and spirit in both the short and long term.

When you start to invite more pleasure, more joy, more spontaneity and more presence into your life on a daily basis, the need for a bit blowout will subside.

The Drink Less, Be More philosophy isn't only about how to have the best nightlife. It's about how to live your best life.

HUSTLE BREAKS
As we discussed in the last chapter, it is essential to find moments throughout the day to rest, to bring yourself into the present moment, and to rejuvenate.

We spend so much time stuck in our minds, which is what makes the allure of using alcohol to turn our brains off so much more appealing.

Floral and plant-based essential oils work wonders, as these scents both connect us to earth energy in a very grounding way and also stimulate the limbic system for a fast-track to pleasure feeling. David Crow of Floracopeia suggests putting a few drops of lavender, rose, geranium or orange blossom oil into your palms, rubbing your palms together and cupping around your nose, and inhaling deeply. This works wonders for an immediate, pleasurable and grounding "brain break."

EAT THE RAINBOW

I'm not talking about a bag of skittles here! Eating a fresh, colourful whole foods diet will entice your taste buds and bring pleasure to your palate, in addition to the health benefits. Joshua Rosenthal, founder of the Institute for Integrative Nutrition and one of my mentors, says: "Eating a wide variety of colors is excellent for your health – the phytonutrients that give fruits and vegetables their lovely hues also enhance bodily functions and prevent illness".

WEAR THE RAINBOW

Adding colour to your wardrobe is a great way to remind yourself to be playful and not take yourself too seriously. Red symbolizes confidence and can help boost your self-esteem, orange suggests creativity and energy, and yellow offers warmth, optimism, and light. If wearing an item of clothing in one of these colours feels too bold, try an accessory that will help remind you of these qualities. If it's a stressful day, and you feel like you might need to soothe your nerves, blue is a calming hue and green helps connect you to nature.

LAUGHTER BREAKS

When I was consumed by my career and on a constant mission for self-improvement I took myself way too seriously. I would only watch educational or informative documentaries, read non-fiction or personal development books, and use my supposed down time to think about "important things" or at the very least, write lists of everything I should be doing. It's no wonder that I needed to get obliterated to turn off my overactive brain.

When I finally committed to healing and creating new habits, I got reacquainted with humour. Silly, fun, playful humour. I also learned that the benefits of laughter are far reaching. Did you know that in addition to releasing endorphins, your body's feel-good chemicals, laughter also relaxes the body, releases stress, improves cardiovascular health as well as strengthens the immune system.

My go-to when times are hard are the Ellen Degeneres Show. I once watched an entire season of reruns, doling them out of an hour a day of diversion - Ellen's ability to combine silliness, cuteness-overload and altruism is genius. I'm also a big fan of baby animal videos - there's a reason "baby panda sneezing" has more than 2 million views!

Other suggestions include spending time with children, checking out the humour section in your local bookstore (I find going to bookstores is also therapeutic in and of itself), hosting a games night with friends or going to a laughter yoga class.

> "Your sense of humor is one of the most powerful tools you have to make certain that your daily mood and emotional state support good health."
>
> — PAUL E. MCGHEE, PH.D.

NATURE BREAKS

Speaking of nature - getting outside and communing with Mother Earth is a great way to ease your stress and add more play during the week. Richard

Louv, author of the bestsellers "Last Child in the Woods" (2005) and "The Nature Principle" (2011) says that a lack of time in nature affects "health, spiritual well-being, and many other areas, including [people's] ability to feel ultimately alive."

Can you eat your lunch in the park? Ride your bike to work and take a route that leads you through the forest? Meet a friend for coffee to go and sit by the ocean, lake or even a pond?

DANCE BREAKS

"Wanting what is only found on the dance floor. The way there I can forget myself, forget my mind and just be my body. Be in it. Become it. Find myself in the losing". - Jeanette LeBlanc

Losing and finding myself in the music used to be my "MO." At the age of 18 I worked at nightclubs, raves, after hours parties and festivals for any opportunity to be surrounded by music, dancing and fun.

I loved it when the music was so loud I couldn't think. There were times during my 20s that I was out 4-5 nights a week, even while working regular full-time jobs.

I still love to dance but have replaced the all-nighters with salsa and bachata, taking classes and going to "baile sociales." At these events, the dance comes first, and alcohol, for the most part, seems to be an afterthought. When I was going through a period of intense healing - and one of my first big breaks from alcohol - I got into Nia dance, so much so that I trained to be a teacher.

Now, I do the majority of my dance breaks in the kitchen, bedroom or office. I've learned that I don't need copious amounts of alcohol or other drugs to effectively move myself out of my head and into my body. Dance breaks are where it's at - and sometimes it only takes a 3-5 minute song to completely shift my mood.

SWEAT IT OUT

As cheesy as it may sound, dancing, cardio, and sweating are a fast way to release those endorphins and get a great natural high happening.

Erin Stutland is the founder of the Shrink Sessions, which combine a mix of yoga, cardio, dance, kickboxing, meditations and affirmations that were created to open your heart, expand your mind and tone your body. "You don't need to put on an expensive pair of Lululemon Wunder unders or be a fancy yoga studio to do it," Erin writes, "All it really takes is 5 minutes. Yes! 5 minutes can create a dramatic shift in state of mind and how you feel about your body."

Erin offers free "Say it, Sweat it, Get it" challenges that deliver high intensive 5 minute videos to your inbox every day. Having followed along several times, I know first hand the ability these 5 minutes have to transform your mindset, reduce stress and get you buzzing on endorphins.They will help prevent you needing that massive blowout on the weekend.

FIND NEW WAYS TO CELEBRATE!!

When I look at Jennifer Lopez, I see a confident, intelligent, accomplished, beautiful woman - who, despite her crazy driven work ethic, seems to be having a lot of fun. I follow her Instagram, and she always appears to be finding ways to celebrate and have fun.

Did you know that the health conscious star avoids drinking alcohol? In an interview with "In Style" Magazine, she says, "I think that it ruins your skin. Of course, during celebratory toasts, everybody's like, 'You can't toast with water!' So I'll toast with alcohol and just take a sip."

Unlike many celebrities we see in the tabloids, her choice didn't stem from a problematic relationship with alcohol, it was a decision she made for her health and appearance.

Most of us don't have the bazillion dollar budget that JLo has to play with. That being said, we can take a page from her book and celebrate with fabulous outfits, meals out with girlfriends, sensual salsa dancing, spa treatments, massages and planning getaways or staycations to exclusive locations.

DAILY SELF-CARE

Self-Care is a vital part of The Drink Less Be More Philosophy and has to do with self-love and acceptance, which are the antidotes to anxiety and stress (both of which plagued me for years). The strategies I've outlined here became easier for me to follow as my daily practice of radical self-acceptance and self-love became a substantial part of my life. Why do I refer to it as radical? Because it was, and is, a complete overhaul, exhaustive at times, thorough, profound and yes, revolutionary.

I used to think of self-care as continuing business as usual (and by that I mean busy-ness as usual), carrying on my work hard/play hard ways, and then treating myself to a massage or mani-pedi every once and awhile. I still see this pattern with so many of my friends and clients. They work work work work work, do do do do do. Eventually the need to blow off steam or release stress becomes so great that a wild night ensues, leading to blackouts, regrets, and inevitably more stress. Overcome by guilt, shame or embarrassment the next day (or whenever the hangover wears off), they beat themselves up with a stricter exercise regimen or pile on more work to make up for the time they feel they've lost. Sound familiar? Yeah, it was my story too for quite some time.

What I didn't realize for so many years is that self-care means taking consistent action to prioritize my health and happiness. To get to a place where I could do this, I had to accept that I was worth it. To accept that I was worth it, I had to love and accept myself enough to make myself a priority (this is where the action steps in Chapter 2 are oh so important). It also took becoming completely burnt out to realize that my modus operandi of work hard play hard simply wasn't working for me anymore. I needed to invite more balance into my life.

This realization deepened when I listened to Dr Christiane Northrup speak at an Institute for Integrative Nutrition conference in New York. She spoke about how addictions and addictive behaviours (such as overworking, over-drinking and over-eating) are the solutions to unresolved pain and trauma. She went on to say that "self-love is an inside job - a radical act." I took this as an affirmation of the need to do the deep, inner healing work necessary before trying to "fix" my outside behaviour.

Elizabeth DiAlto, founder of the Wild Soul Movement (which empowers women to get out of their heads and into their bodies), advocates "self-acceptance before self-improvement." I often see my clients get stuck when their concept of self-care is just another task to be checked off their to-do list, and often confusing self-care for self-improvement. "Exercise, check. Meal prep, check. Visualization to envision the goals I want to achieve, check."

When I recommended scheduling and prioritizing more self-care to one of my clients, she responded, exclaiming back to me "what the heck is self-care anyway?? And don't tell me all I need to do is to meditate more!!"

She has a point. It is not my place to suggest exactly what self-care should mean to another person. You have to figure that out for yourself.

For this client, self-care included bringing more joy into her life, and riding her bike several times a week. For another client, it was signing up to a boxing gym and doing cardio dance classes. The point is to do several things a week that make you feel great.

Focus on what truly nourishes your body and soul, what brings you joy and pleasure and feels like fun to do. Challenge yourself to slow down and create space in your busy schedule. As Elizabeth DiAlto wrote in a recent blog, "Space is crucial to feeling calm, peaceful and making good choices."

Some of the many practices that are regularly a part of my self-care practice include

- a daily meditation practice
- a delicious, healthy and non-negotiable morning routine (water and lemon, green tea or mate, stretching and meditation, green smoothie or juice, journaling, and gratitudes
- beautiful candles and a plethora of sensual body oils and aromatherapy oils
- rituals around letting go what of what no longer serves me
- affirmations and the Thrive Threesome (see Chapter 2 for a refresher)
- dance and other forms of sexy, fun exercise
- lots of time in nature
- bubble baths, massages, and saunas

SLEEP

I call myself a reformed chronic under-sleeper. I have suffered a compromised immune system and what I would now consider to be fairly serious memory loss as a result. I now know that the importance of including sleep in your "Be More" repertoire is a must. The Harvard Women's Health Watch reports that being chronically underslept can lead to weight gain, high blood pressure, and a decrease in the immune system's power.

To get the most out of life, one has to have the energy, vitality, stamina and a healthy, happy mindset. By sleeping the recommended amount of at least 7 hours per night, you are setting yourself up for Drink Less Success by reducing stress, increasing your positive mood and mindset, controlling your weight, building a strong immune system to fight off illnesses and diseases, and improving your memory.

If you often have a hard time falling to sleep, consider developing a bedtime routine that helps you wind down. Avoid caffeine for at least 6 hours before bedtime, drink soothing teas, have a bubble bath or do some meditation or gentle stretching. Create a soothing ambiance with candles and aromatherapy, and switch off technology (yes, that includes your phone). And of course, avoid drinking alcohol to put yourself to sleep. We now know that while you may fall asleep faster, your sleep will be more fitful and less restful if you are relying on alcohol to help you unwind.

ACTION STEPS:

1. Write a list of everything that helps you feel good in your body and at peace in your mind.
   How do you want to feel in your life?
   What qualities do you want to invite in?
   What energizes you? Excites you?
   What brings you deep relaxation?
   What helps you get out of your head and into your body?
   What helps you blow off steam and release stress?
2. Now, get out your calendar or day planner and start blocking off time weekly to prioritize your self-care.

Conclusion

I t took me burning out of my lifestyle and a good 4+ years of healing, recuperating, learning and eventually thriving and supporting others to do the same, to be able to share this guide with you.

The stories and strategies included in this guide are meant to empower and support you to take small, actionable steps. Start redefining your "work hard/play hard" programming and your relationship to alcohol, and start living life in the most full and fun way possible, and wake up hangover free.

I believe that you can have it all. You can play every day, live a wildly adventurous and exciting life and treat your body like a temple. Making the healthiest choices possible for your "now," and your future.

Change isn't always easy, and if it were, it probably wouldn't be so rewarding. Remember that the action steps are there for a reason - to take action - and by taking consistent action you can start to create new habits.

If you feel overwhelmed, or worried that you aren't going to be able to follow through, know this: I believe in you. I have faith that you can make the changes that you want to make. I see your future, and it is bright.

Sometimes it feels like the forces against us are greater than we are; our friends, colleagues, bosses, clients, the media, popular culture, sometimes even our families, girlfriends or boyfriends... all telling us what normal looks like. But now you know differently, don't you? You can create a new normal for yourself, one that gives you the results you desire, for your health and happiness - based on your desires for yourself.

Start by making one small change, then another. Try a new strategy each week, or each time you go out. You set yourself up for success when you make small changes one at a time. Remember that there are no failures, no 'messing up." Everything is a chance to learn more about yourself. You are a pioneer. You're learning as you go; you are creating a new path for yourself, which is very brave.

Use this guide to empower you and to help you take control of your alcohol use. Say goodbye to feeling stuck, shame spirals and mornings of regretful "oh no not agains..." once and for all.

Say hello to increased energy, focus and fun. Say hello to feeling confident, empowered, and in control of your life. Say hello to more clarity, vibrancy and confidence.

Let me know how it goes for you. I would love to hear what works best for you, what your unique challenges are and whether there are other strategies you'd like to see explored and developed in the next edition of this guide. You can email me directly at drinklessbemore@caitlinapdgett.com

Make sure to access your bonus resources - including my favourite recipes and extra hot tips - at www.caitlinpadgett.com/drinklessbemore

When to get additional help

If you have tried the strategies in this guide or have tried periods of abstinence to no avail, it may be time to stop for a moment and more deeply assess your relationship to alcohol. Why? Because if you are experiencing addiction or physical dependence to alcohol - there are other places to get support first, before this guide will work for you. This guide is full of amazing strategies you can use if you want to try cutting back. However, if you have a more serious issue with alcohol, it is essential you seek the right kind of support.

Take a moment to answer the following questions honestly:

1. Do you need increasing amounts of alcohol to produce the desired effect?
2. Do you experience any of the following withdrawal symptoms: tremors, anxiety, sweating, agitation and restlessness, nausea, and diarrhea? Do you feel depressed or have trouble sleeping when you don't drink? Does drinking more alcohol relieve these symptoms?
3. Does drinking occupy a higher priority than other interests, hobbies or obligations?
4. Do you often crave or feel triggered to drink alcohol? If you have one drink, do you always want to drink more?

5. Are you aware that you should drink less, yet despite your best efforts, you always seem to drink more than you intended?
6. Have you experienced repeated negative consequences while drinking, yet despite your knowledge of what might happen, you continue to do so?

If you answered yes to any of these questions, you might want to consider additional support.

If you feel you might be in need of additional support, I can help you find the options best suited to your situation.

Email drinklessbemore@caitlinpadgett.com and let me know. Your email will always be kept confidential.

Acknowledgments

I t seems incredible that so many people influenced the writing of this little guidebook. It is because this guide is both personal and also a representation of my professional focus. So many people helped me "get here" - to this place where writing and sharing this guide has become a reality.

To my clients: you show up bravely to do this work and create a new reality for yourselves, even when it's terrifying. You are proving to yourself and others that you can be in control of alcohol, that you can define the terms, and that you can live a life so full of purpose, joy and success that alcohol feels like an afterthought. Thank you for trusting me with your stories.

To my accountability partners: Nyssa Tan and Heather Wise, without both of your dedication to showing up even when the going got tough, unconditional support and honest feedback as content editors, I wouldn't have completed this book. That's a fact. I'm deeply grateful to you!

To my content editors: you helped me feel confident and ready to share this book publicly. Each brought their own set of expertise and experience, and am deeply indebted to each other of you for taking the time out of your busy schedules to give such wonderful feedback and edits. Thank you Aleka Heinrichi, Natalie Chan, Jillian Kowalchuk, Brandy Svendson, Kyla Zanardi, Nicola Judkins and Dove Sussman.

To my research assistant: Jillian Kowalchuk, you stepped in at the perfect time to save me from overwhelm. It was very important to me that this book was more than opinion-based. Thank you for helping source the evidence for the effectiveness of moderation.

To my copy editors:

Aoife O'Leary! You were able to take my wordy, run-on, stream of conscious first few Chapters and craft concise paragraphs and action steps - no small feat! You affirmed my voice and helped me stay consistent and true to myself through the entire book- and that is a huge gift. Thank you for sharing this journey with me.

Jan Padgett, aka my mom, your attention to detail and the finer points of grammar were challenged while reading this draft! I appreciate where you challenged me, and encouragement to me uphold the highest standard in my recommendations and guidelines. More importantly, I appreciate the fact that I could share this draft with you without being scared of feeling judged. It speaks volumes to our relationship now.

To my mentors:

I am deeply grateful to those who have shaped my evolution with inspiration and loving kindness, and sometimes tough love. Some I have met in person. Others have answered questions at conferences and event and their responses have directly shaped the next steps I felt confident in taking. Others have authored books that have transformed me, and given me words and concepts to articulate my own experience.

Dara McKinley - finding you, Nia, and the Goddess Process (before it had been named) gave me permission to desire and dream big. I hope to dance with you again, dear friend.

Marie Forleo - receiving a scholarship and attending RHH Live was one of the defining moments in my life. Your commitment to supporting women to share their gifts with the world and the community you have created through B-School has been a huge part of my evolution. You also introduced me to the work of Kris Carr!

Kris Carr - when I hearing you speak at RHH Live in 2010 changed my life. I didn't have a cancer diagnosis but I certainly needed a wake up call. When you spoke about your fast-paced, stressed-out life and the impact it had on your health, it was like you were shining light into the parts of me I wasn't quite ready to acknowledge yet. Your book, Crazy Sexy Diet, inspired the kind of information delivery I wanted to achieve within my community: smart, well-researched, funny and frank. Plus, you talked about alcohol moderation on the basis of health but allowed room for your readers to decide which path was the best one for their life and experiences.

Todd Herman - you were also at RHH Live. I asked a question, something to do with not feeling supported by the community I was a part of at the time, and you responded with a no BS, no beating around the bush respond to the effect of "Maybe it's time you found new friends." I took that to heart, seeking friendships with those who would see my light and support me to shine.

Danielle LaPorte - you always to find the words to express the truths I want to share. You inspire me to be a better writer and speaker, to embody the qualities of elegance, eloquence, and accessibility... no small feat! The Desire Map, the idea of locating the feeling and going for that feeling no matter what, and developing goals with soul are something I share with my clients time and time again.

Brene Brown - Your work on shame and vulnerability has been so profoundly impactful for myself and my clients, I often share your Ted talks in my newsletters and your books as gifts to my clients. More recently, I appreciated about reading about your commitment to storytelling in the introduction to Rising Strong. You inspired the nascent qualitative researcher in me (to be continued...)

Gabby Bernstein- I didn't really "get" the concept of spirituality as it related to sobriety until I hear you speak about sobriety as a connection to spirit. Your story has inspired thousand of women, I'm sure. I'm definitely one of them. As you wrote in Spirit Junkie, **"Everything you've always wanted will come to you when you get sober."** This became true for me when I decided never to get drunk again.

Rachel Luna - it was in your group Thrive and Hustle that I first spoke the words "I have a book I want to write about women and alcohol." Speaking those words aloud, and receiving your enthusiast support, firmly implanted the idea in my head.

Kristen Domingue - when we first spoke, I was afraid to step fully into my story and own my purpose. It was more of a "someday" idea. You gently and firmly pulled away my layers of self-doubt and helped me see that I had everything I needed to do this work. Moreover, that this work was so needed, that it was my duty not to wait. You knew that this was my purpose, my unique gift. Thank you for helping me see it.

Jina Schaefer and Carla Golden - connecting with you both early on in my business was so crucial. I was scared to be so open and vulnerable and you both reached out with cyber hugs and support. Carla, when I you first shared your writing with me, I hadn't yet been exposed to many health coaches who were writing about alcohol so candidly. Jina - your 40 day challenges on Facebook are always amazing to be a part of, and documentation of your 100 days alcohol free inspired me as I was stepping into this world online world of coaching.

Tommy Rosen - It is likely you have no idea the impact you have on the thousands of people from around the world listening to the Recovery 2.0 Online Conferences. In the past couple of years, I have learned about the power of plants and essentials oils, meditation and yoga, nutrition, sexual healing, spirituality and more. I love the holistic approach to supporting people to thrive in their recovery. Thank you for making these options available.

Dr Christianne Northrup - I was so thrilled to hear your speak at IIN Live in New York. Finally, the woman behind the life-changing "Our bodies, our lives" - up close and personal! Little did I know that the content of your speech would be so bang-on to the work I was about to launch into the world. I loved how you described the process of recovery as "remembering who you are in the first place" and how addictions and addictive behaviours are the solution to the unresolved pain and trauma that so many of us carry with us into adulthood. Thank you for affirming that self-love is a radical act.

Arianna Huffington - Hearing you speak at IIN Live and subsequently reading your book Thrive was another transformative experience for me. In addition to Dr Northrup's emphasis on self-care, you really brought home the importance of sleep and rest, and how getting enough of both is a radical act in today's hustle society. You inspired me as a writer; I connected to your style of sourcing content - valuing to a variety of experiences, whether it be an anecdote from your mother or sister, or a research study, or a song.

Joshua Rosenthal - I believe that inherently knew and understood the concept of bio-individuality from a young age. When I was in a youth advocacy program, and we were taught the "just say no" approach to alcohol, drugs and sex, it didn't sit right with me. My 10 year career in harm reduction in sexual health and drug policy was about "meeting people where they are at" - finding the best option for each individual based on their unique set of experiences, their personal goals and desires. When I enrolled in IIN, it felt like coming home. The approach to a bio-individual approach to health and the emphasis on primary foods for healing are so transferable to working with dependencies external to oneself. The combination has been perfect for me and my clients.

Lindsey Smith - Your commitment to The Launch Your Dream Book Course has been unwavering. Thank you for your passion, devotion and expertise. Without you, and the LYDBC, this book would never have come to fruition in less than 6 months!!

And finally, to my daughter Luna Azul who is my daily motivation, and Luis, who gave me the foundation of love and support for this all to have been possible.

References

Introduction

The Center for Disease Control and Prevention reports that... Esser MB, Hedden SL, Kanny D, Brewer RD, Gfroerer JC, Naimi TS. Prevalence of Alcohol Dependence Among US Adult Drinkers, 2009–2011. Prev Chronic Dis 2014;11:140329. DOI: http://dx.doi.org/10.5888/pcd11.140329

Buddha describes the middle way... http://www.sgi.org/about-us/buddhism-in-daily-life/the-middle-way.html

The middle is messy...
Brown, Brene. Rising Strong. Spiegel & Grau, 2015. Kindle edition: location 436

Though studies demonstrate that moderation is possible... http://www.doctordeluca.com/Library/AbstinenceHR/HRforAlcProbs02.pdf
http://www.moderation.org/

Chapter 1: "I can't do this anymore" Setting New Intentions: Visualizing a "new you"

Intention is the starting point...
5 steps to setting powerful intentions, Deepak Chopra MD, retrieved from Deepak Chopra Centre September 29, 2015, http://www.chopra.com/ccl/5-steps-to-setting-powerful-intentions

Danielle LaPorte, creator of The Desire Map...
Why I gave up chasing goals, Danielle LaPorte, retrieved from HuffPost Healthy Living.
Posted: 12/13/2012 EST Updated: 02/11/2013
http://www.huffingtonpost.com/danielle-laporte/chasing-goals_b_2270936.html

Our intention creates our reality...
The Power of Intention: *Learning to Co-create Your World Your Way*, by Dr. Wayne W. Dyer
Hay House, 2005

Chapter 2: "But what if I can't change?" The Power of Positive Thinking: Building the belief that change IS possible for you

Brene Brown, whose research and stories...
"I thought it was just me: Women reclaiming power and courage in a culture of shame" Brene Brown, http://brenebrown.com/books/

Dr Masaru Emoto, a researcher and alternative healer...
Retrieved from Yoganonymous. com June 2015 http://yoganonymous.com/watch-scientific-proof-that-our-thoughts-intentions-can-alter-the-world-around-us

Even our worst enemies...
Thrive, Arianna Huffington. Harmony Books. 2014. p. 155

Kristen Domingue, my former coach... http://kristendomingue.com/

Gabrielle Bernstein, best-selling author...
Thanksgiving Gratitude, Giving and Gorging, HuffPost Healthy Living, Posted: 11/23/2011 Updated: 01/23/2012
http://www.huffingtonpost.com/gabrielle-bernstein/thanksgiving-gratitude_b_1105213.html
To learn more about Gabby's work visit: http://gabbyb.tv/

Martin Seligman, Robert Emmons, and Michael McCullough are three scientists...
The importance of Gratitude. UMass Dartmouth. Retrieved June 2015. http://www.umassd.edu/counseling/forparents/reccomendedreadings/theimportanceofgratitude/

Dara McKinley... The Goddess Process http://daramckinley.com/
Regena Thomashauer, aka Mama Gena's School of the Womanly Arts...
http://www.mamagenas.com/

Danielle LaPorte... http://www.daniellelaporte.com/

Martha Beck... http://marthabeck.com/

Chapter 3: "What if I mess up?" Creating Accountability Strategies to support you as you change

Todd Herman, a business management consultant..
Retrieved July 2015 from the article Developing Personal Accountability, https://www.mindtools.com/pages/article/developing-personal-accountability.htm

One of my favourite slogans from the Al-Anon meetings... http://www.al-anon.org/

Gretchen Ruben, self-professed happiness expert...
Better than Before: Mastering the Habits of our everyday lives, Gretchen Ruben, Crown Publishing Group, 2015
For more information on Gretchen's work, visit: gretchenrubin.com

Marie Forleo - if it's not scheduled, it's not real... retrieved from http://www.marieforleo.com/
Chapter 5: "How will I actually do things differently?" Same Party, Different You

Follow Dr Oz's Low Risk Drinking Guidelines... Retrieved from http://www.oprah.com/health/Alcohol-and-Your-Health-Dr-Ozs-Rules-for-Safe-Drinking

As Terri Cole, a well-respected psychotherapist and coach writes...
The secret to being confident, retrieved August 2015 http://www.positivelypositive.com/2013/08/16/the-secret-to-being-confident

Alcohol switches off an antidiuretic hormone... retrieved July 2015 from What to eat before, during and after a night out, by Dale Pinnock, November 2013 http://www.telegraph.co.uk/men/active/10428463/What-to-eat-before-during-and-after-a-big-night-out.html

Chapter 6: "What will my life be like?" How a Great Night can equal a Great Life

Nutrition and wellness tips...
http://www.ion.ac.uk/information/onarchives/thinkbeforedrink
http://kriscarr.com/products/crazy-sexy-diet/

http://www.integrativenutrition.com/iin-book-excerpt
http://www.davidwolfe.com/
http://www.foodrenegade.com/how-beat-sugar-cravings-glutamine/
http://www.tommyrosen.com/yoga/
http://thedailylove.com/how-i-overcame-addiction/

Thích Nhất Hạnh, The Miracle of Mindfulness: An Introduction to the Practice of Meditation, Beacon Press, 1999

Priming... Tony robbins interview with Marie Forleo http://www.marieforleo.com/2014/12/tony-robbins/

Julia Cameron, the creator of the Artist's Way...
Morning pages: http://juliacameronlive.com/basic-tools/morning-pages/

Chapter 7: "Do I have to do this alone?" Communication and Relationship

FOMO - In my drinking days... Retrieved from Addiction.com, written by Kelly Fitzgerald, "The Sober Señorita" The Phenomenon of "FOMO" and the Alcoholic August 19, 2015
http://www.addiction.com/expert-blogs/the-phenomenon-of-fomo-and-the-alcoholic/

Chapter 8: "The thought of sober sex freaks me out" Alcohol and Intimacy: Once you change you'll never go back!

As Rebecca Reid challenges... Retrieved from The Telegraph, "Sober Sex Takes Balls of Steel but It's Worth It" Rebecca Reid, March 2015
http://www.telegraph.co.uk/women/sex/11444253/Sober-sex-takes-balls-of-steel-but-its-worth-it.html

According to a study by the American Psychology Association... Testa, Maria; Collins, R. Lorraine, Alcohol and risky sexual behavior: Event-based analyses among a sample of high-risk women. APA. 1999

Something we don't actually hear about often... Alcohol & Sex, Brown University, Retrieved August 2015 from:
http://brown.edu/Student_Services/Health_Services/Health_Education/alcohol,_tobacco,_&_other_drugs/alcohol/alcohol_&_sex.php

Selected Strategies in Chapters 7 and 8 adapted from:
http://summertomato.com/8-tips-for-drinking-less-without-your-friends-knowing/
http://www.cosmopolitan.com/sex-love/advice/a7212/things-not-to-say-to-a-non-drinker/
http://www.cosmopolitan.com/lifestyle/a6969/partying-in-late-twenties/
http://www.cosmopolitan.com/sex-love/advice/a27290/best-things-about-not-drinking/
http://www.succeedsocially.com/avoiddrinking

Chapter 9: What about binges and blackouts? Your body and your brain

The National Institute of Alcohol Abuse and Alcoholism (NIAAA)... "Drinking levels defined," retrieved July 2015 http://www.niaaa.nih.gov/alcohol-health/overview-alcohol-consumption/moderate-binge-drinking

Dr Jonathan Chick, of the Alcohol Problems Service at the Royal Edinburgh Hospital... Retrieved from article in the Guardian, "Regular Binge Can Cause Long-term Brain Damage" December 29, 2008 http://www.theguardian.com/society/2008/dec/29/binge-drinking-brain-damage-study

Another interesting study, conducted by Chris and Alexander van Tullekens... Retrieved from the the Daily Mail, "What's really unhealthier - binge drinking or a small daily tipple? The results of this unique experiment - by identical twin doctors - will surprise you" PUBLISHED: 18 May 2015, UPDATED: 19 May 2015

http://www.dailymail.co.uk/health/article-3086908/What-s-really-unhealthier-binge-drinking-small-daily-tipple-results-unique-experiment-identical-twin-doctors-surprise-you.html#ixzz3oHN7FISu

In a National Institute for Alcohol and Addictions publication on alcohol and Alzheimer disease... Tyas, Suzanne, "Alcohol Use and the Risk of Alzheimer Disease" Retrieved July 2015, http://pubs.niaaa.nih.gov/publications/arh25-4/299-306.htm

Dr Fulton T. Crews, professor in the Department of Pharmacology and Psychiatry at the University of North Carolina... Retrieved from Medill Reports, Emily Wasserman, January 23, 2013, "One day of binge drinking linked to brain damage, researchers say" http://newsarchive.medill.northwestern.edu/chicago/news-214412.html

Kris Carr, Crazy Sexy Kitchen... 5 tips to reduce inflammation, Retrieved July 2015, http://kriscarr.com/blog-video/5-tips-to-reduce-inflammation/

Studies show that the atrophy of brain cells decreases after abstinence from alcohol... Retrieved from "Alcohol's Damaging Effects on the Brain" http://pubs.niaaa.nih.gov/publications/aa63/aa63.htm

Jina Schaefer... To read more about her work and 40 day Alcohol Free challenges: www.jinaschaefer.com

Stick to the recommended daily amount... Canada's Low Risk Drinking Guidelines, Canadian Center on Substance Abuse, http://www.ccsa.ca/Resource%20Library/2012-Canada-Low-Risk-Alcohol-Drinking-Guidelines-Brochure-en.pdf

As Dr Michael Wilks says... Retrieved June 2015 from Drink Aware UK, "How much alcohol is too much?" https://www.drinkaware.co.uk/check-the-facts/what-is-alcohol/how-much-is-too-much

Katie Corcoran, Founder of Thrive and Hustle... to learn more about her work: www.katiecorc.com

Geneen Roth, who writes on the topic of bingeing in relationship to food... Retrieved from "Binge Trance: Interrupted" https://geneenroth.com/2014/02/23/binge-trance-interrupted/

Sarah Hepola, author... "Blackout: Remembering The Things I Drank To Forget" Grand Central Life & Style (23 June 2015)

In her article "Anatomy of a Blackout" Julie Beck writes... Retrieved from The Atlantic, June 17, 2015 http://www.theatlantic.com/health/archive/2015/06/blackout-book-memoir-science-sarah-hepola/395909/

Additional resources for this Chapter:
CDC binge drinking defined: http://www.cdc.gov/alcohol/fact-sheets/alcohol-use.htm

We need to talk about our drinking: http://www.theglobeandmail.com/life/health-and-fitness/health/we-need-to-talk-about-our-drinking/article19377132/

The difference between men and women: http://oade.nd.edu/
educate-yourself-alcohol/alcohol-and-women-critical-information/
differences-between-men-and-women/

Problem Drinker Defined: http://alcoholrehab.com/alcoholism/
problem-drinker-defined/

Chapter 10: "What if work hard/play hard is my 'mo'?" Developing a Drink Less be More Life Philosophy

David Crow of Floracopeia... Retrieved from Recovery 2.0 Online Conference. For more information on Floracopeia: www.floracopeia.com
For more information on Recovery 2.0: www.tommyrosen.com/yoga/

As Joshua Rosenthal, founder of the Institute for Integrative Nutrition says... http://www.integrativenutrition.com/iin-book-excerpt

Your sense of humor... Paul E McGhee quote, Retrieved from "Laughter is the best medicine, health benefits of laughter" http://www.helpguide.org/articles/emotional-health/laughter-is-the-best-medicine.htm

Richard Louv, author of the bestsellers "Last Child in the Woods" (2005) and "The Nature Principle" (2011) says... Retrieved from National Geographic Article "Connecting With Nature Boosts Creativity and Health" By Brian Clark Howard, PUBLISHED JUNE 30 2013, http://news.nationalgeographic.com/news/2013/06/130628-richard-louv-nature-deficit-disorder-health-environment/

Wanting what is only found on the dance floor... Jeanette LeBlanc, retrieved from Facebook. To learn more about Jeanette and her writing, please visit: www.peacelovefree.com

Erin Stutland, founder of Shrink Session... Quote retrieved from newsletter, June 23, 2014. To learn more about Erin's work, please visit: www.shrinksessionworkout.com

Elizabeth DiAlto, Founder of The Wild Soul Movement... quote from "Sensual Practices For Feeling Calm And Peaceful In A Hectic And Crazy World" www.wildsoulmovement.com/calm

Dr Christiane Northrup... quote retrieved from IIN Live conference presentation March 2014, to learn more about Dr Northrup's work, please visit: www.drnorthrup.com

The Harvard Women's Health Watch... retrieved from "Importance of Sleep : Six reasons not to scrimp on sleep" http://www.health.harvard.edu/press_releases/importance_of_sleep_and_health

Made in the USA
Middletown, DE
11 May 2016